Cromosys Publication

Teach Yourself Microsoft WORD

NIRANJAN JHA SHOWMAN

Cromosys Publication

Teach Yourself Microsoft Word

NIRANJAN JHA SHOWMAN

Founder - Niranjan Jha Showman

Education and Technology Research Center

Patankar Park, Nallasopara (W), Mumbai. +91-9561450045

Education, Technology, Publication, Healthcare, Newsmedia, Realtor, Filmmaking

www.facebook.com/cromosys

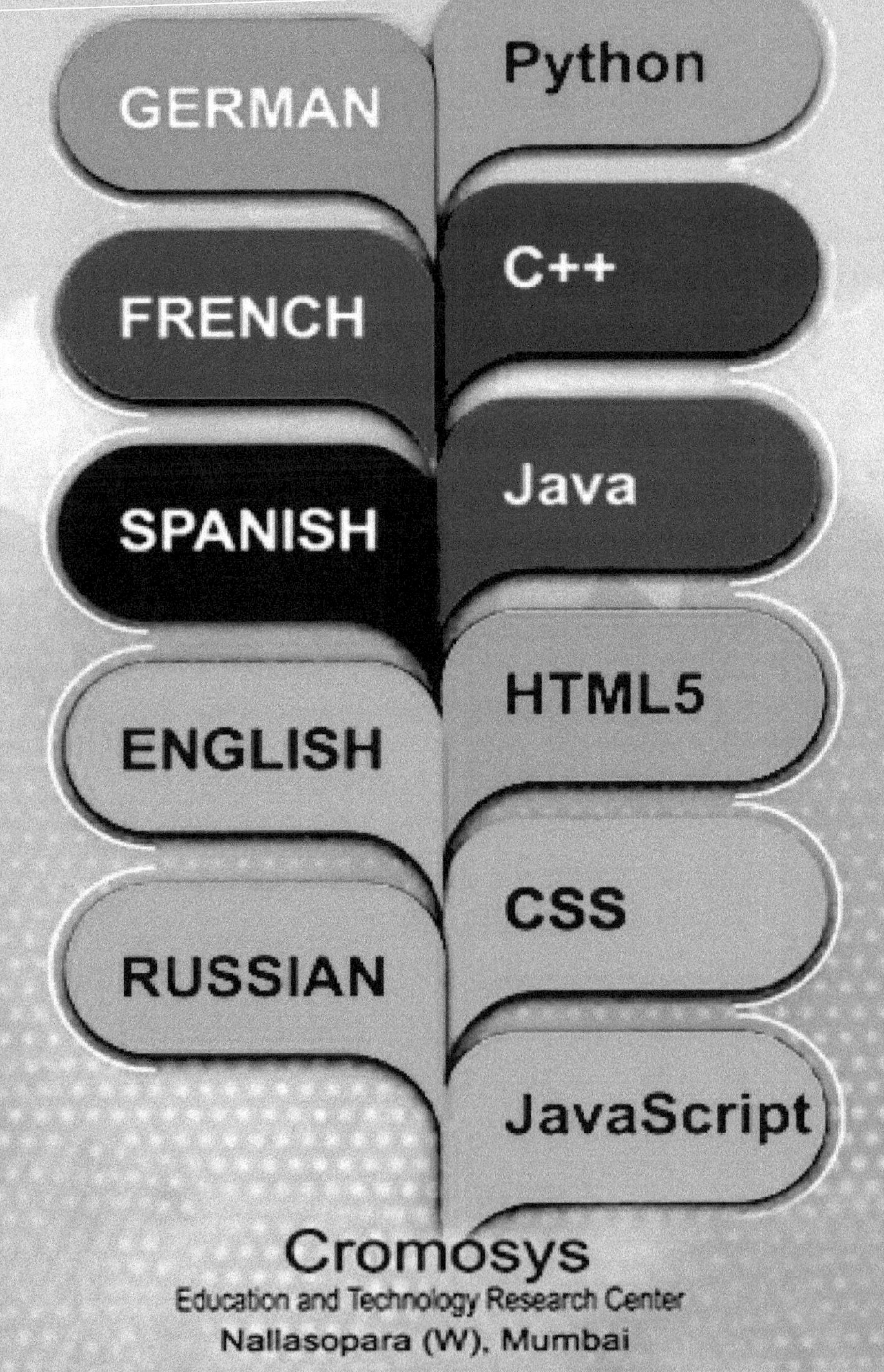

+91-9561450045
Learn Advanced Skills
And Get Job Instantly
GERMAN
Python
FRENCH
C++
SPANISH
Java
ENGLISH
HTML5
RUSSIAN
CSS
JavaScript
Cromosys
Education and Technology Research Center
Nallasopara (W), Mumbai

Learn Web Programming
Demo-Class Free
HTML
CSS
React
JavaScript
Typescript
Bootstrap
Cromosys
20 Years of Experience
Nallasopara (W), Mumbai
+91-9561450045

+91-9561450045
Learn Software Engineering
Demo-Class Free

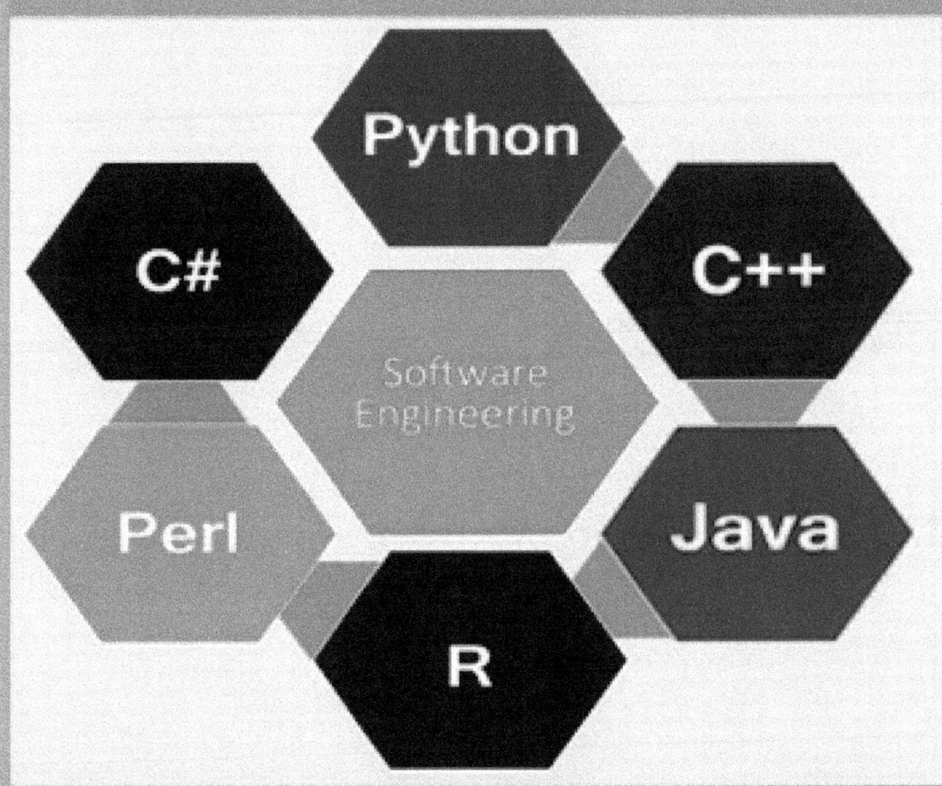
Python
C#
C++
Software
Engineering
Perl
Java
R

Cromosys
20 Years of Experience
Nallasopara (W), Mumbai
+91-9561450045

25 Years of Experience
Learn Visual Multimedia
Animation VFX
Movie Editing
Game Development
Cromosys
+91-9561450045
Education and Technology Research Center
Nallasopara (W), Mumbai
www.facebook.com/cromosys

JoB
Jobs Available
For Candidates Who Know
German
French
Spanish
Vacancy in Germany, France, Spain
For Hospitality, Engineering, IT Sector
With Free Visa, Airfare and Accommodation
Cromosys
Education and Technology Research Centre
Nallasopara (W), Mumbai
+91-9561450045
20 Years of Experience

+91-9561450045
Foreign Languages Institute
German, French, Spanish
Basic and Advanced - All Levels
3 x 6 = 18 Courses
FRANCHISE
Business Offer
Teaching Materials Provided
We have 1 Million Students Globally
Great Income Assured
Global Exposure
Cromosys
20 Years of Experience
Nallasopara (W), Mumbai
+91-9561450045

Book: Teach Yourself Microsoft Word
Author: Niranjan Jha Showman
Publisher: Cromosys Publication
ISBN: Acquired
Date: 2020
Category: Computer Education

Preface

Some people say that Microsoft Word is so easy that there is no need of any book to learn this program. What they say is right, but do you know one thing? They have never known how big Microsoft Word is, and what are the advanced commands associated with this application. For example: Hyperlink, Mail Merge, protecting a document with password, locking a document so that no one can even open it, locking the entire folder, saving as PDF, and saving as Web page. These are the advanced commands in Microsoft Word which help you understand this application thoroughly and completely. And so, we have explained about all these commands, and have given the steps with pictures in this book. Cromosys Publication's **Teach Yourself Microsoft Word** book is an optimal quality guide to the beginners and advanced learners of Microsoft Word 2013 and the latest version. We are the leading book publisher of languages and technology. Our research and education center working for last fifteen years has made tremendous efforts to simplify the learning of Microsoft Word, and so we assure you that this book will walk you through in the simplest way in your entire course of learning, and will make you a master of Microsoft Word application in just one month of time. This all-inclusive book provides you with in-depth knowledge of word processing program with various steps and examples. An easy-to-understand, step-by-step approach, supplemented with practical implementation and many real-life screenshots are some of the distinguishing features of the book. The lessons conceived and prepared by us will help you start learning from real basic making your move amazing, astonishing, and exhilarating for you. It's cool, simple, and sublime!

Niranjan Showman, the author of this and fifty other books published online, is the founder, and owner of Cromosys Corporation. His dedication in technological and linguistic research is significantly known to millions of people around the world. This book is the creation of his avowed determination to make the learning of Microsoft Word easy to the people. After you install the application on your system, you just have to follow the instructions of this book doing the same on your computer, and you will see that you are quickly learning everything. Just an hour of practice per day, and in a month of time you'll get a lot of knowledge, tips and tricks to work with this software. This is an unmatchable unique book of its kind that guarantees your success. The lessons are magnificently powerful to bring you into the arena of word processing. With the industrial growth from the year 2014, the accurate and profound knowledge of this software has influenced millions of minds; therefore we conceived the idea of making this book a guideline to those who want to be perfect in this application starting from real basic.

Cromosys education system is intelligently dedicated to our avid and passionate readers, predominantly acknowledging and appreciating the fact that they are on the path of making a career in the respective domains. Each Cromosys book is designed to ensure that in addition to gaining the requisite theoretical knowledge, the readers gain sufficient hands-on practice and practical knowhow to master the nitty-gritty of the profession. Since Microsoft has revolutionized the working experience on personal computers with its office automation applications, due to the interactive user-interface and simplicity of use, Microsoft Word gained popularity very quickly. Microsoft Word 2013 is one of the most sophisticated word processing programs available today. With this application, it is easier than ever to efficiently create a wide range of business and personal documents, from the simplest letter to the most complex report. It includes many desktop publishing features that you can use to enhance the appearance of documents to make them more appealing and readable. Microsoft Word 2013 has been completely redesigned to make it user friendly so that even a novice user can work on it efficiently. This version of the application includes all of the functions and features in a more organized way. This interface is easier to learn because it is more logical and visual.

Cromosys, our education and technology research center, saving human efforts from being wasted, is committed to help you gain profound and contemporary knowledge. The world growing with density has brought enormous opportunity to computer professionals irrespective of their geographical boundaries. We strongly believe that this book is useful to all who work on Microsoft Word. After you start the lesson, you don't need to worry about anything but just follow each and every step carefully. This book is designed to fulfill the instant need of learners in a very economical way, as it is easy to find on Internet and affordable to buy and share. Cromosys, our path-breaking pioneer training institute for Computer Courses, English Speaking, Foreign Languages, and Competition Coaching, is dedicated to enlightening human mind with educational endeavors, and we are doing the same for last successful fifteen years. And recently we have come up with 'Worldwide Online Teaching System' for languages and technology. We not only hope but believe that your success is in your hand, as this book will take you miles ahead in your expectation. We always respect the views and comments of readers, so for any communication with regards to assistance, enquiry or collaboration, we are always there at your reach as it helps us improve our quality.

Niranjan Jha Showman
Founder: Cromosys Corporation
Web: facebook.com/cromosys
Contact no.   +91-9561450045
Email address: cromosys@yahoo.com

Books by the same author:
Teach Yourself Microsoft Excel, Teach Yourself Tally, Teach Yourself Adobe Premiere Pro CS6, Teach Yourself Adobe Flash, Teach Yourself Adobe Dreamweaver, Teach Yourself Autodesk Maya, Teach Yourself Autodesk 3ds Max, English Voice Accent and Pronunciation, English Word Power, English Dictionary of Modern Slang, Teach Yourself Spanish, Teach Yourself French, Teach Yourself German

Cromosys
Education and Technology Research Center
Education, Technology, Publication, Healthcare, Realtor, Filmmaking
Nallasopara (W), Mumbai, India

Caution: All the writing works that include all the educational, non-educational books, novels, and articles of the author Niranjan Jha, are the registered contents of Online Digital Services and also published contents of his registered magazine FACE OFF - Inventing Truth, which carries registration no. MAHENG12112/13/1/2009-TC and the endorsement no. 3244 28/5/2009 with the Ministry of Information and Broadcasting, Govt. of India. Any plagiarism in this regard will attract strict legal action. Any further publication of any of his books requires his written permission. Copyright certificate of this book is attached at the end of this book.

Lesson 1
Introduction

Microsoft Word is a word processing program and it is a part of the Microsoft Office suite. It is a basic program used worldwide for typing, content editing, and letter drafting. After you install this application with Windows operating system on your computer, you can open this program. MS Word has tabs and ribbon interface that makes the features easy-to-use. Perform the following steps to open MS Word:

1. Click the **Start** button present in the <u>Taskbar</u> of your desktop screen.

2. Select **All Programs** option from the Start menu, and then select **Microsoft Office**.

3. Select **Microsoft Word 2013** from the sub-menu. As the result, the MS Word application window appears on your screen, as shown in picture 1.1.

Picture 1.1

About MS Word Options

MS Word has merged all the dialog boxes into a single massive Word Options dialog box which is called Office Button. This button is located at the top-left corner of the MS Word screen. Perform the following steps to view the Office Button dialog box:

1. Click **Office Button** at the top-left corner of the MS Word screen. It opens a dropdown list on the screen.

2. Click the **Word Options** button which is at the bottom of the dropdown list. As the result, the Word Options dialog box appears, as shown in picture 1.2.

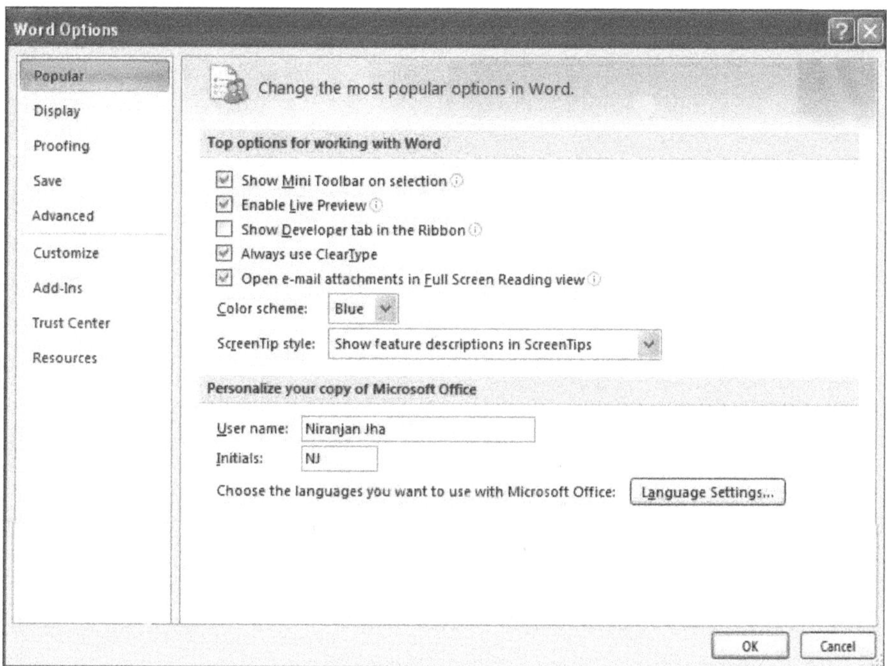

Picture 1.2

You can see in this picture that the left pane of the Word Options dialog box shows the options grouped in tabs. The setting associated with each tab is displayed in the right pane. You can close this dialog box after viewing it. Remember that you can press **F1** key for Help anytime while working in Word. It opens a help screen where you can search the content of help, or you can type the keyword of the help topic.

Closing the Document

You should always make sure to save a document before closing it. You can save the document by clicking the save icon located in the Quick Access Toolbar. This toolbar is at the top-left of the MS Word screen. You can also save the document by selecting Save option from the dropdown list of the Office Button. We will discuss in detail about the Save option in the next lesson. Here we need to learn about closing the document. Perform the following steps to close the MS Word document:

1. Click **Office Button** at the top-left corner of the MS Word interface. It opens the dropdown list on the screen.

2. Select the **Close** option at the bottom of the dropdown list. As the result, the Word document is closed.

If you have done any change in your document without saving, then a dialog box is displayed. It asks whether or not you with to save the changes to your document. You can save the changes by clicking the Yes button or else click the No button.

Exiting from MS Word

After closing the document, you can exit from the MS Word program. Let's perform the following steps to exit from the Word application:

1. Click the **Office Button** to open the dropdown list.

2. Select the **Exit Word** button which is at the bottom-right of the dropdown list. As the result, the Exit Word button closes the Word application.

Shortcuts of Lesson One

Shortcuts are used to perform the steps quickly on the computer. You can use several shortcuts in Microsoft Windows operating system for MS Word. Following is the list of some shortcuts that you can use for MS Word program:

- To open Microsoft Word:
  Click **Start** button, select **Run**, type: **winword** in Run box, and click **OK** button at the bottom.
- To open Microsoft Word:
  Press **Windows key** which is beside Ctrl key on the keyboard. Then press **P** key to select All Programs and press **Enter**, then press **M** key to select Microsoft Office and press **Enter**, then **arrow down** to Microsoft Office Word and press **Enter**.
- To close Microsoft Word:
  Press **Alt+F4** keys together on the keyboard to close the Microsoft Word program.
- To close Microsoft Word:
  Click the **X button** at the top-right of Microsoft Word screen.

Lesson 2
User Interface of MS Word

Since the early 90s, the user interface of MS Word has remained unchanged. However, there was a growing need to redesign MS Word to give it a totally new look and enhanced and user-friendly features. Therefore, Microsoft designed a completely different user interface Word 2013, to address this concern. In this interface, the menus and toolbars are replaced by a new tab and ribbon interface that makes the features easy-to-use. Let's get familiar with some of the interface features of MS Word with the help of following points:

Quick Access Toolbar: This toolbar is at the top-left corner of the MS Word screen. It contains the commands that are most frequently used, such as save, undo, and repeat.
Title Bar: This bar is at the very top of the MS Word screen. It shows the name of the document that you have currently opened.
Minimize/Maximize/Close buttons: These buttons are at the top-right corner of the screen. These buttons perform the three basic operations, such as minimizing, restoring, and closing the document.
Tabs: The seven tabs namely: Home, Insert, Page Layout, References, Mailings, Review, and View organize various commands of the Word document into groups.
MS Word Workspace: It is a white page in the middle of the MS Word screen. It allows you to type the desired text on the Word document.
Rulers: Refers to the margins that represent the writable region in the Word document.
Scroll Bars: These bars are at the right and at the bottom of the MS Word screen. These bars are used to scroll the word document vertically and horizontally.
Status Bar: This bar is at the bottom of the MS Word screen. It displays information, such as total page count, present page number, and total number of words, of the presently open document.

Accessing and Customizing Quick Access Toolbar

In MS Word, Quick Access Toolbar appears just beside the right of the Office Button on the Title Bar. The fully customizable Quick Access Toolbar displays icons that represent commonly used commands such as Save, Undo, and Repeat. You can add and remove commands in Quick Access Toolbar according to your requirement. The picture 1.3 shows the Quick Access Toolbar at the top-left corner.

Picture 1.3

In addition to Save, Undo, and Repeat commands, the toolbar has a Quick Access Arrow. It is a downward pointing arrow with a hyphen on the top. You can use this arrow to customize Quick Access Toolbar. Let us now learn to use the Quick Access Toolbar commands with the help of the points mentioned below:

- **Save:** Allows you to save currently open document. If you are saving a new file, the Save As dialog box appears and you have to provide a name to your file before saving it.
- **Undo:** Allows you to undo the last action. In addition, you can click the downward pointing arrow beside the Undo command to display a list of one or more of your previous actions.
- **Repeat:** Allows you to reverse the last Undo command. This command helps you to repeat the action done by the Undo command.

Quick Access Toolbar is designed to group commands that you often use while working in Microsoft Word. In addition to default commands, you can add or remove other commands available in the dropdown list of Quick Access Toolbar. Perform the following steps to add other command icons to Quick Access Toolbar:

1. Click the **Customize Quick Access Toolbar** arrow to open the dropdown list.

2. Click the icon name, such as **New** or **Quick Print** from the dropdown. The icon name gets selected and appears in Quick Access Toolbar.

You have learnt to add command icons to Quick Access Toolbar. Now if you want, you can remove them as well. Perform the following simple steps on your computer to remove an icon from Quick Access Toolbar:

1. Right-click an icon on **Quick Access Toolbar** to open a dropdown list.

2. Click the **Remove from Quick Access Toolbar** option from the dropdown list. As the result, the selected icon is removed from Quick Access Toolbar.

Title Bar

The topmost bar on the MS Word window is the Title bar, as shown in picture 1.3. When you open the MS Word window, the Title bar shows the name of the document and its type. You can also drag the Word window by using Title bar. By default, the Title bar shows Document1 – Microsoft Word as the name of the document. The Title bar of Word 2013 contains the Office Button, Quick Access Toolbar, Minimize, Maximize/Restore and Close button.

Minimize/Maximize/Close Buttons

When you are not using a window, you can minimize and remove it temporarily from the screen. When you minimize a window, it appears as a button on the Taskbar. You can find the Minimize button at the top-right corner of the MS Word window.

Now when required, you can display the minimized window again on the screen by clicking the corresponding button on the Taskbar. As the result, the window reappears on the screen in its previous size. In addition, if you want to view the document window on the full screen of your computer, then click the Maximize button on the Title bar.

You can close the currently displayed document by clicking the Close button located in the Title bar. When you close an unsaved document, a dialog box appears asking you to whether or not save the document before closing.

Working with Tabs

In the new MS Word, all the menus have been replaced with the tabs. There are seven main tabs in MS Word, which are as follows: Home tab, Insert tab, Page Layout tab, References tab, Mailings tab, Review tab, and View tab. Let's learn in detail about these tabs one by one.

Home Tab

The Home tab contains the basic operations related to text and paragraphs. These operations are divided under different groups. It also has various predefined styles to change the appearance of the text. The Home tab with various options is shown in picture 1.4. Below the picture, the table provides brief information about the various groups of the Home tab.

Picture 1.4

Groups of the Home Tab

Group Name	Purpose
Clipboard	Offers options to cut, copy, and paste the text, and use Format Painter.
Font	Contains commands to change the appearance of your text. You can also click the option button to open the Font dialog box, which contains most of the font settings.
Paragraph	Allows you to indent, align, and justify paragraphs; create bulleted and numbered list; change spacing; add borders and shading; sort text; and view special characters. You can also click the option button to open the Paragraph dialog box.
Styles	Provides you with the preset formatting that helps you keep your Word document consistent.
Editing	Allows you to find and replace text. The options of this group also allow you to select objects.

Insert Tab

In addition to text and paragraphs, you may need objects, such as pictures, ClipArt, and SmartArt, in the document to make the document more interesting and lively. You can insert these objects with the help of the Insert tab. The Insert tab with various groups is shown in picture 1.5. Below the picture, the table provides brief information about the various groups of the Insert tab.

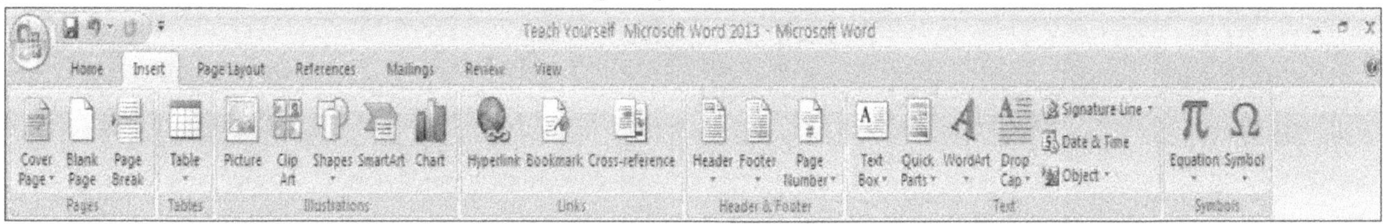

Picture 1.5

Groups of the Insert Tab

Group Name	Purpose
Pages	Allows you to add a cover page, blank page, and page break to your document.
Tables	Lets you draw a table, insert an Excel spreadsheet, or add a predefined table into your document.
Illustrations	Lets you add pictures, ClipArt (images included in MS Office), shapes, SmartArt (diagrams), and charts to your document.
Links	Lets you create links to websites (called hyperlinks) and other places (for example email) in your document (bookmarks and cross-references).
Header & Footer	Allows you to enter the text at the top or bottom of each page, respectively. This group lets you add a header, footer, or simple page number. On the other hand, when you click one of these options, you get a menu of preset choices. That means you can add a header, footer, or page number with just two clicks.
Text	Offers you a menu of stylish text boxes by clicking the Text Box command. You can also draw a blank text box. You can insert building blocks and document properties, such as turning words into art; creating a larger capital letter at the beginning of a paragraph; adding a signature line to your document; and inserting the current data and time and another file into your document.
Symbols	Lets you add symbols and equations. When clicked, each item displays a menu of choices. You can see that inserting a complicated equation is an easy task.

Page Layout Tab

The Page Layout tab contains the commands that are related to the page. Using this tab, you can select the predefined themes; set margins, size, indentation, and spacing of the text in the page. These all affect the layout of the page. The Page Layout tab with various groups is shown in picture 1.6. Below the picture, the table provides brief information about the groups of the Page Layout tab.

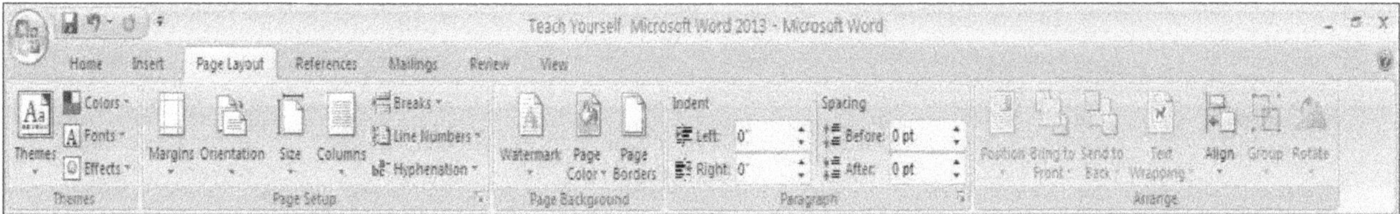

Picture 1.6

Groups of the Page Layout Tab

Group Name	Purpose
Themes	Lets you select an overall theme for your document, which includes color, font, and effects of the document and text.
Page Setup	Allows you to set the margins, orientation, page size, page columns, page breaks, line numbers, and hyphenation.
Page Background	Controls what goes on your page, behind your text. You can select a watermark, solid color, or page border.
Paragraph	Controls paragraph indent or spacing. You can also open the Paragraph dialog box using the option button at the bottom-right corner.
Arrange	Lets you arrange objects on the page. The examples of objects are pictures, ClipArt, WordArt, and text boxes.

References Tab

The References tab contains a number of commands, such as Table of Contents, Footnotes, and Citation & Bibliography. In addition, it contains the Caption commands that are used to give captions to figures and diagrams. The picture 1.7 shows the various groups of the References tab. Below the picture, the table provides brief information about the groups of the References tab.

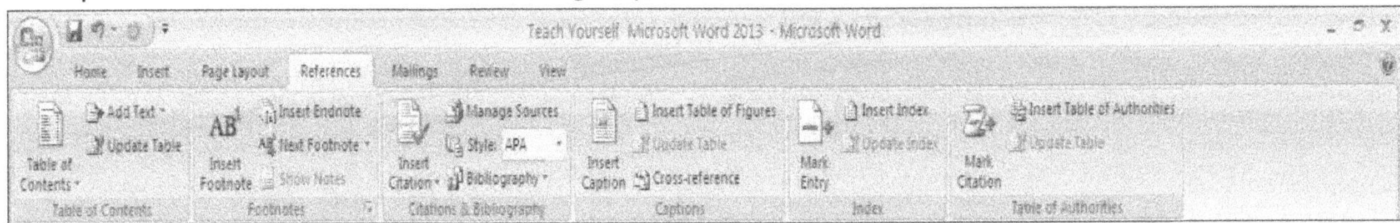

Picture 1.7

Groups of the References Tab

Group Name	Purpose
Table of Content	It deals with the table of contents. (A table of contents is listing of chapters and other significant titles in your document. You can select a style for your table of content, and text to it, and update it.
Footnotes	Allows you to insert footnotes and endnotes in the document. If you have ever read or prepared a formal report, or written a term paper, you would know all about footnotes and endnotes. Numbered notes are added to the end of every page (in the case of footnotes) or document (in the case of endnotes).
Citation & Bibliography	Allows you to insert citations and bibliographies in the document. Citations and bibliographies are another item often found in formal reports or papers. The information about a publication is called a citation and a number of citations are called a bibliography.
Captions	Allows you to insert captions underneath a graphic (such as a picture or table). The captions help in indentifying a graphic. The commands in this group help you insert captions and cross-references (references to other places in your document); and create a table of figures (a list of graphics in your document).
Index	Lets you mark a word for the index as well as insert and update the index. An index is a list of topics that are covered in a book and the page numbers where those topics can be found.

Table of Authorities — Allows you to mark a citation, create a table of authorities, and update the table. A table of authorities is usually appears in legal documents, as they reference cases and statutes. The Table of Authorities group helps you create this kind of reference page.

Mailings Tab

The Mailings tab has the commands and options, which are used to create documents, such as envelopes, letters, and labels that you can mail. It commands are focused on mail merge, which is a process that takes a form letter and list of contacts and creates a personalized message for each recipient. The picture 1.8 shows the various groups of the Mailings tab. Below the picture, the table provides brief information about the groups of the Mailings tab.

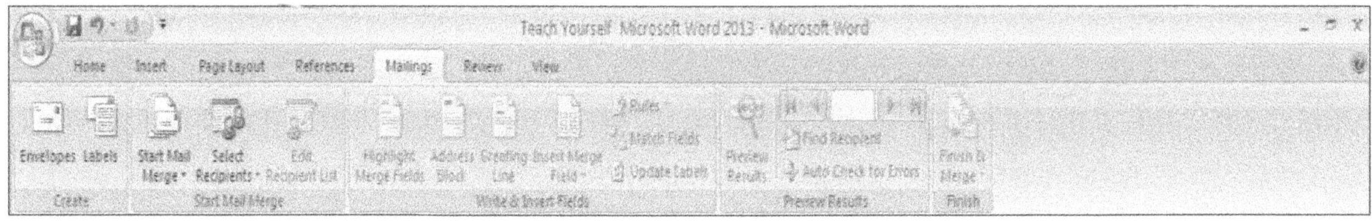

Picture 1.8

Groups of the Mailings Tab

Group Name	Purpose
Create	Allows you to create envelops and labels. When you click the Labels or Envelopes command, it opens a dialog box. You can use this dialog box to create different types of envelopes and labels, as per your requirement.
Start Mail Merge	Allows you to compose a message for mass e-mailing or distribution. The Start Mail Merge group is where you can start creating a mail merge. You can select the type of merge you want to perform as well recipients of email.
Write & Insert Fields	Allows you to add the different customizable portions of your document (called fields). The commands in the Write & Insert Fields group are used after you complete the mail merge process.
Preview Results	Lets you preview your results before you finish the merge. As you can see, you can also navigate through the records, find a recipient, and check for errors.
Finish	Opens a menu that provides you options to finish the mail merge.

Review Tab

The Review tab contains the commands used to review the document. This tab provides you an option to compare the document and protect your document from unauthorized users. The picture 1.9 shows the various groups of the Review tab. Below the picture, the table provides brief information about the groups of the Review tab.

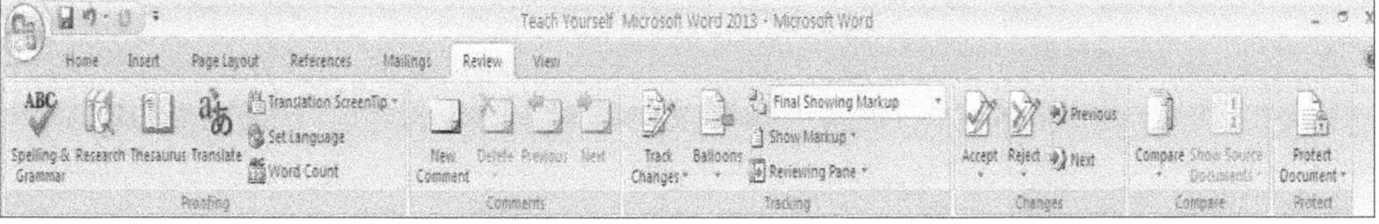

Picture 1.9

Groups of the Review Tab

Group Name	Purpose
Proofing	Contains commands to check spelling, perform research, look up words in the thesaurus, translate words, set language, and perform a word count.
Comments	Lets someone add easily identifiable ideas and thoughts to the document. This group lets you create, delete, and navigate through comments.
Tracking	Refers to the feature of track changes, which is helpful in cases when a document is reviewed by multiple reviewers. This feature lets you have every change to the document recorded. It is very useful for editing purposes. This group lets you enable, disable, and control the back change feature.
Changes	Lets you accept, reject, and navigate through tracked changes that have been made to your document.
Compare	Lets you compare and combine documents. This Compare group is very useful when you have multiple versions of documents.
Protect	Offers a menu that allows you to restrict access and changes to your document. You can open the menu by clicking the Protect Document.

View Tab

The View tab contains command through which you can view your document in different ways. It also contains macros through which you can record some action and repeat that action anywhere in the document. The picture 2.0 shows the various groups of the View tab. Below the picture, the table provides brief information about the groups of the View tab.

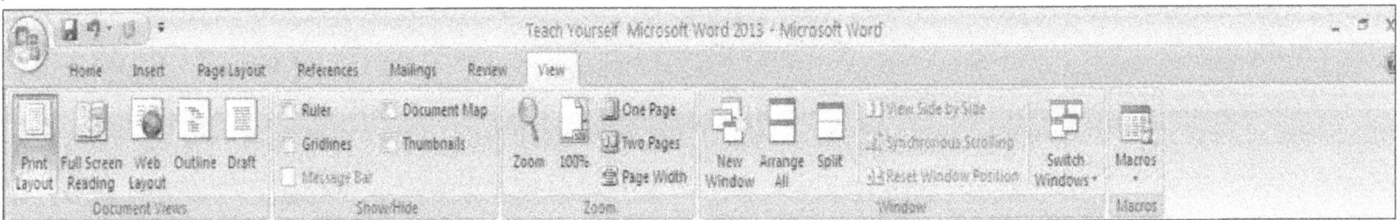

Picture 2.0

Groups of the View Tab

Group Name	Purpose
Document Views	Refers to the group, which lets you view your document in different ways. For example, when you click the Print Layout option, you can see your document as it appears on the paper.
Show/Hide	Refers to the group, which contains items that can be hidden or shown on the screen. You can check the icons, which you want to view on the screen.
Zoom	Refers to the group, which contains a host of functions. The Zoom button opens a dialog box to select specific zoom settings. The next button automatically sets your zoom level to 100%. The next three buttons zooms to show one page, two pages, and the page width.
Windows	Refers to the group, which contains three columns. The commands in first column are used to create a new window, arrange windows, or split the current window. The second column of commands lets you view documents side by side and control how they appear. The last command is Switch Windows, which lets you switch between open documents.

Macros   Refers to the group, which lets you open the Macros dialog box. If you click the dropdown arrow, you would see a menu related to macros. Macros let you record or code a series of commands so that you can perform a number of actions with just a few clicks.

The MS Word Workspace

Workspace is a white-page working area inside the document in which the text, graphics, WordArt, and tables are inserted. You can work directly on the Workspace from the place from the place where the cursor is located. A cursor is a moving marker or pointer that indicates the position in a workspace.

Rulers

In MS Word workspace, the rulers contain margin indicators that represent the right, left, top, and bottom margins.

Scroll Bars

Scroll bars are used to move the page in a window. This bar provides the ability to scroll vertically and horizontally through a document. You can scroll the horizontal bar to left and right and vertical bar to up and down to see the text that is beyond the visible screen. You can scroll one line at a time by clicking the single arrows located at the top and bottom of the scroll bar. You can scroll through a full screen by clicking the shaded area above or below the location indicator.

Status Bar

The Status bar is located at the bottom of the MS Word window. It is divided into sections, and each section shows different information about the document. Its main purpose is to display the information about the current state of a document. The Status bar from left to right shows the number of pages in the document, number of words in the document, proof reading errors, different views of the document, and zooming options.

Lesson 3
Preparing the First Document

When you start preparing a Word document, you need to take care of numerous issues regarding the document. For example, you need to set the page margins and size of the document. Further, you are required to decide the typeface and font size of the document. After that, you need to format the document to make it readable and user friendly. Further, you need to customize the document as per your requirements. If required, you can change the background of the document.

This chapter makes you familiar with the ways to format the text and pages in a Word document. This chapter presents the techniques to set the size, margins, and orientation of the document. Further, you learn to type the text and insert symbols, equations, and hyperlinks in the document. In addition, you learn to insert numbered and bulleted list and table in a Word document. Finally, you learn to save and print the document. Let's first start with what should be considered before we start preparing a Word document.

Consideration before Preparing a Document

When you open MS Word, you see a blank document that covers most of the space of your computer screen. This space is known as workspace. In the workspace, you may wonder where to start from. However, there are certain things related to page and text settings that you must consider before preparing your first document, which are listed as follows:

- Setting the page margins
- Setting the size of the document
- Setting the orientation of the page
- Setting the font and font-size of the text

Setting the Page Margins

Page margins are the empty spaces along the left, right, top, and bottom edges of a page. Headers and footers fall in the top and bottom margins, respectively. In addition, you can put graphics, text boxes, and page numbers in the margins. Margins serve to frame the text and make it easier to read. MS Word 2013 offers you various types of page margins. By default, the Normal margin is configured by MS Word.

Setting the Size of the Document

By default, the standard size of a document is 8.5" x 11". However, you can print your document in various other sizes, such as legal and letter size. There are several types of document sizes available in MS Word. The size of document also includes the height and width of the document. You can select any kind of size as per your requirement.

Setting the Orientation of the Page

MS Word provides two types of orientation to a document namely, Portrait and Landscape. The Landscape orientation is the one in which the width of the page is more than its length like a painting of a scenery. Generally, the documents are printed in the Portrait style. In the Portrait style, the document is oriented with the short margins on the top and bottom of the document. However, a document oriented in a Landscape looks very different from a usual document. You can use the Landscape orientation mostly when you have text or an image that is too wide to fit across the page in Portrait orientation. Few reasons to use the Landscape orientation are wide images, table with many columns, or image and text wrapped together.

Selecting the Font and Font-size of the Text

A font is a collection of letters, numbers, and symbols in a particular typeface. It includes all italic and boldface variations of letters, numbers, and symbols. The look of the text is determined by its fonts, the size and color of the letters, text effects, and font styles. Font styles include boldface, italic, underline.

Setting Size, Margin, and Orientation of a Document

You can set page margins, document size, and orientation of the document by selecting the options provided in MS Word. In addition, you can apply different sizes and styles of fonts in your document as per your requirement. This makes the document more readable, well structured, and organized.

Setting the Page Size

There are in-built page sizes available in MS Word 2013. Perform the following steps to set a page size of your choice:

1. Click the **Page Layout** tab at the top of the MS Word screen. It opens a number of groups with numerous options in the Ribbon.

2. Click the **Size** button in the <u>Page Setup</u> group, as shown in picture 2.1 with the red arrow. It opens a dropdown list on the screen.

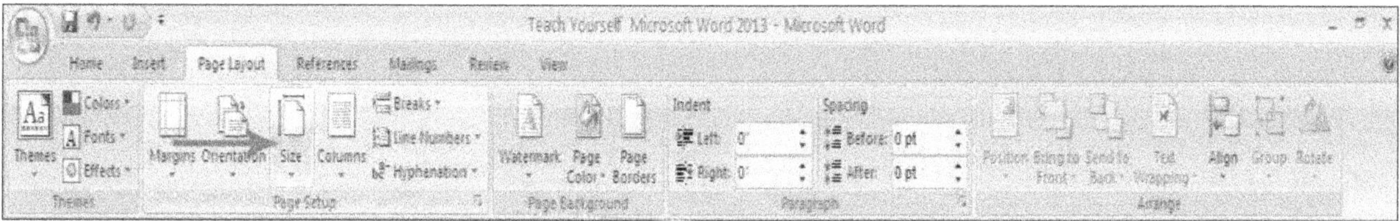

Picture 2.1

3. In the dropdown list, **click** the desired page size. In our case, we select **A4** page size, as shown in picture 2.2. As the result, the document appears as per the selected page size.

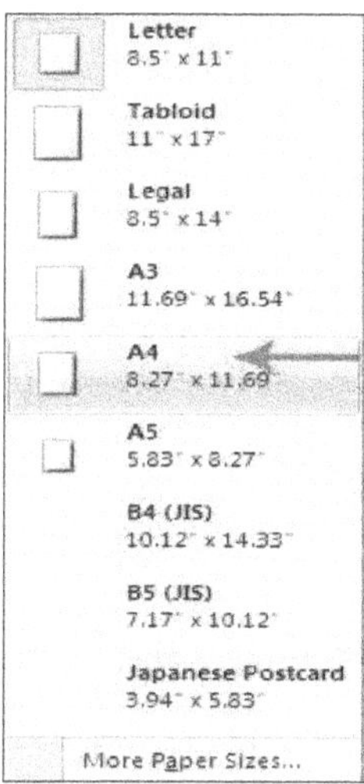

Customizing the Page Size

Microsoft Word allows you to customize the page size. You can do it by clicking the Page Setup Dialog Box Launcher button which is under the Page Layout tab. The dropdown list of the size contains all the in-built sizes of the document. You can perform the following steps to change the size of the document as per your requirement:

1. Click the **Page Layout** tab at the top of the MS Word screen.

2. Click the **Page Setup Dialog Box Launcher** button, as shown in picture 2.3. It opens a dialog box on the screen.

Picture 2.2

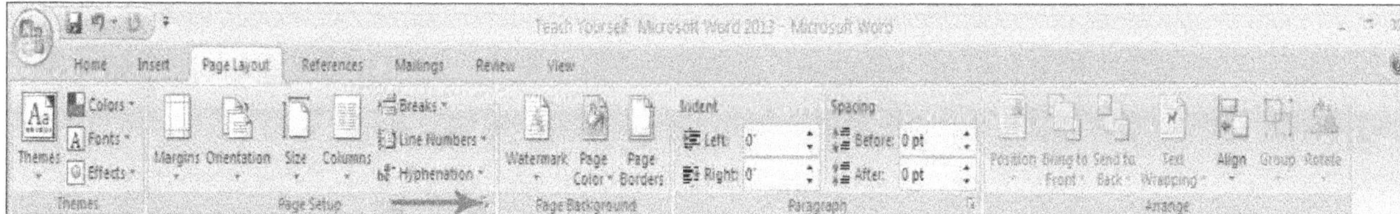

Picture 2.3

3. Click the **Paper** tab in the <u>Page Setup</u> dialog box. Then **enter** your own setting in the <u>Width</u> and <u>Height</u> text boxes, and click the **OK** button to save the changes.

Now you can see on your screen that the document size has been set according to the Width and Height specified in the Page Setup dialog box. Let's learn how to set the margins of the document in MS Word 2013.

Setting Margins

There are in-built page margins available in MS Word. You can select any of the page margins by clicking on it. Perform the following steps to set the page margins:

1. Click the **Page Layout** tab at the top of the MS Word screen.

2. Click the **Margins** button in the Page Setup group. It opens a dropdown list on the screen.

3. **Click** the desired margins from the dropdown list. In our case, we select the Wide margin. As the result, the margins of the page are set according to the size you selected.

Customizing the Margins

A document looks more organized when its margins are properly set. The default margins are usually fine for documents. However, if you require different margin settings for your document, you can change them. MS Word allows you to customize the margin settings for your Word document. The dropdown list of margins contains all the predefined margins that can be used in the document. Perform the following steps to change the margins as per your requirement:

1. Click the **Page Layout** tab at the top.

2. Click the **Page Setup Dialog Box Launcher** button, as shown in picture 2.3. It opens the Page Setup dialog box on the screen.

3. Click the **Margins** tab in the dialog box. Then **enter** values in the Top, Bottom, Left, and Right text boxes.

4. Click the **OK** button to save the changes. As the result, the document margins have been set according to the values specified in the Page Setup dialog box.

Setting Orientation

The page orientation means the layout of the entire document, which specifies how the document would appear on the paper after printing. The default orientation is Portrait, in which the length of the page is more than its width. Most documents, like the pages of this book, are printed in the portrait style, with margins left out of the page on the top and bottom. You can also set the orientation to Landscape, in which the width of the page is more than its length, by clicking the Orientation button and selecting that option. In daily use, the Landscape document is not used. However, sometimes printing in landscape mode is necessary to fit the text, tables, and graphics on a single page. Perform the following steps to set the page orientation:

1. Click the **Page Layout** tab at the top.

2. Click the **Orientation** button to open a dropdown list.

3. Click the **Landscape** option from the dropdown list. As the result, the document appears in landscape orientation.

There are some alternate steps for setting the page orientation. Alternatively, you can also perform the following steps to change the page orientation:

1. Click the **Page Layout** tab at the top.

2. Click the **Page Setup** group button to open the Page Setup dialog box.

3. Select the **Margins** tab.

4. Click the **Landscape** button in the <u>Orientation</u> area.

5. Click the **OK** button at the bottom.

Typing the Text

You can start typing in the document from the position of the cursor. The cursor tells you the place on the page from where you can start typing. The blank spaces that appear on the left and right to the cursor are margins. When you start typing, the page begins to fill from the upper-left corner of the document. When you type text in a document, it is displayed in a particular font. Each font consists of alphabetic characters, numbers, and symbols that share a common design. By default, the font used for the text in the MS Word document is Calibri. However, you can change the font at any time. The available fonts vary from one computer to another, depending on the program installed. Some common fonts include Arial, Verdana, and Times New Roman.

Entering Special Characters while Typing

Some characters especially symbols, such as the copyright symbol (©), can be extremely difficult to type. You can insert any symbol or character from any font by using the symbol dropdown gallery or the Symbol dialog box. In this section, we discuss about inserting a symbol and equation.

Inserting a Symbol

Symbols are special characters that do not appear on the keyboard. These special characters vary from country to country, depending on the keyboard being used and installation language selected for the MS Word. If you are looking for a special character, such as the currency sign for a different country or the copyright or trademark symbol, you can find it in the Symbol gallery. Perform the following steps to insert a symbol in the document:

1. Place the **cursor** in the location where you want to insert a symbol.

2. Click the **Insert** tab. Then select the **Symbol** button under the <u>Symbols</u> group, which is at the right of the Insert menu bar.

3. **Choose** the desired symbol from the Symbol dropdown list, (shown in picture 2.4). In our case, we select the copyright symbol (©). As the result, the symbol is inserted in the document.

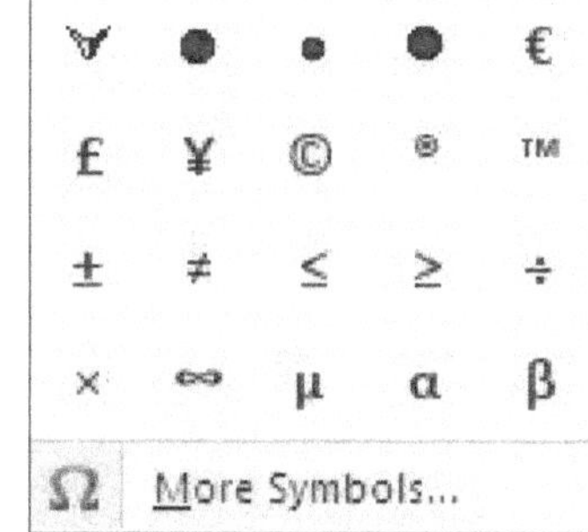

Picture 2.4

The Symbol dropdown list shown in picture 2.4 includes some commonly used symbols. If you are looking for a symbol other than the commonly used symbols, perform the following steps:

1. Click the **Insert** tab at the top.

2. Select the **Symbol** button under the <u>Symbols</u> group in the Ribbon. It opens a dropdown list.

3. Click the **More Symbols** option in the dropdown list. It displays the <u>Symbol</u> dialog box, as shown in picture 2.5.

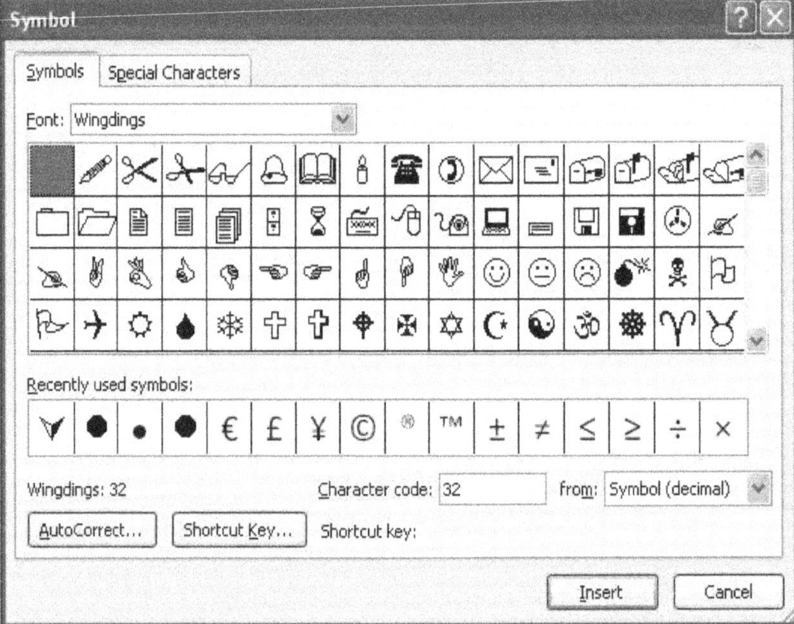

Picture 2.5

4. **Choose** a symbol or foreign character from the <u>Symbol</u> dialog box. You may have to scroll to find the desired symbol.

5. Click the **Insert** button at the bottom of the Symbol dialog box. Then click the **Close** button to close the Symbol dialog box.

If you are looking to insert some more interesting symbols, you can select Webdings or Webdings 1, 2, or 3 in the Font dropdown list.

Inserting a Special Character

You can use the Symbol dialog box to insert special characters, such as registered mark (®) and ellipsis (…) that are not on your keyboard. Perform the following steps to insert a special character:

1. In the <u>Symbol</u> dialog box, click the **Special Characters** tab at the top.

2. **Choose** the desired character, and click the **Insert** button at the bottom of the Symbol dialog.

3. Click the **Close** button in the Symbol dialog box.

Working with an Equation

Microsoft Word 2013 has some preset equations and mathematical structures that you can insert into the Word document. You can access and edit the equations as per your requirements. MS Word 2013 provides several commonly used equations to insert in your document. For example: the equation for binomial theorem and the area of a circle. Let's learn to insert the Binomial Theorem equation into your document:

1. **Place** the cursor at the point where you want to insert an equation.

2. Click the **Insert** tab at the top.

3. **Click** the dropdown arrow beside the Equation button under the Symbol group.

4. Choose the **Binomial Theorem** equation from the dropdown list, as shown in picture 2.6.

As the result, the Binomial Theorem equation is inserted in your document. This equation is surrounded by a blue outline know as Equation Editor, which helps you to edit the equation within the document itself.

5. **Click** anywhere outside the Equation Editor area. Now the equation appears as a normal text.

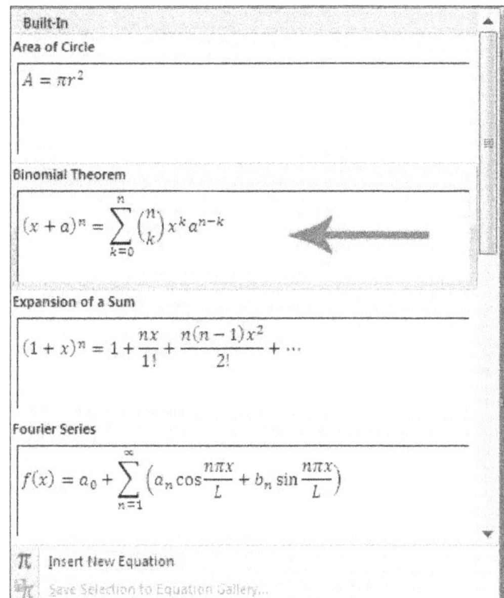

Picture 2.6

Writing an Equation

MS Word 2013 provides you the facility to write an equation as per your requirement. In writing the equation, you can use the integral structure and some symbols, such as = and − sign, from the Symbols group. Perform the following steps to write an equation:

1. **Place** the cursor where you want to insert the equation.

2. Click the **Insert** tab, and **click** the dropdown button beside the Equation button under the Symbols option.

3. Choose the **Insert New Equation** option from the dropdown list. The **Equation Editor** appears on the document screen. In addition, contextual Equation Tools tab appears on the Ribbon at the top.

Now you can type your own equations by using the Equation Tools, if it is not available in the list of equations. The Equation Tools contextual tab is divided into three groups namely: Tools, Symbols, and Structures. All the three groups collectively help the users to create their own equations in the Microsoft Word document.

4. Click the **Equation Editor** box on the document screen and type the equation. In our case, we type an integral equation.

Lesson 4
Working with a Hyperlink

When you click a hyperlink on a Web page, it takes you to a different Web page or different place on the same Web page. A hyperlink is a link through which you can navigate from one place to another in a document or Web site. However, in MS Word, you can use hyperlinks to connect readers to your favorite Web pages or different page, slide, or file. Let's now learn how to insert a hyperlink to link your file with another file as well as create links to Web pages.

Linking a Hyperlink to a Web Page

A hyperlink includes the path information to another object. The objet can be a target on the same document, a file on the same computer, or any location on a Web page. In case of linking to a Web page, the hyperlink includes the path and name of the Web site. Perform the following steps to create a hyperlink to a Web page:

1. **Select** the text of your document to form the hyperlink. You can select a line or phrase for this.

2. Click the **Insert** tab at the top.

3. Click the **Hyperlink** button under the Links group. It opens the Insert Hyperlink dialog box, as shown in picture 2.7.

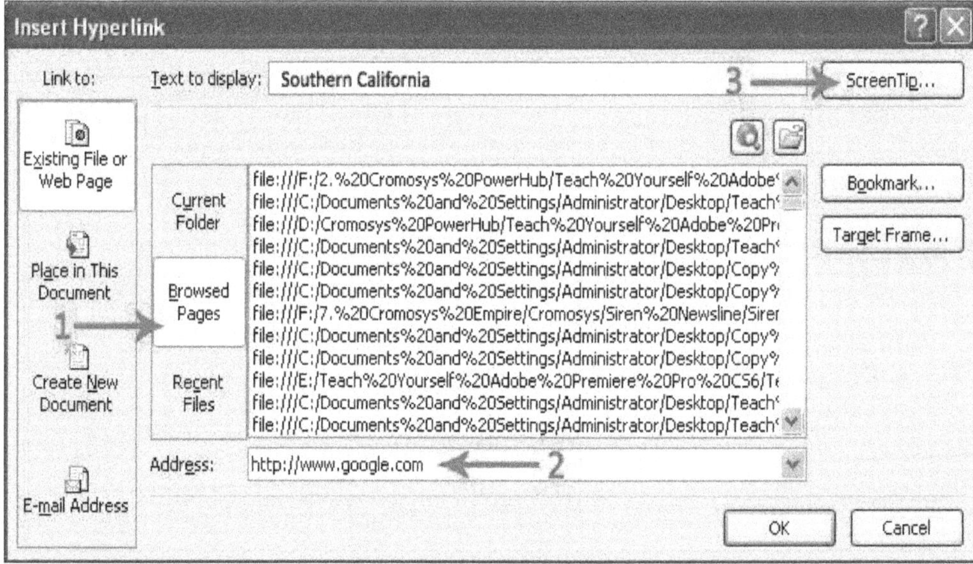

Picture 2.7

4. Click the **Browsed Pages** button in the Insert Hyperlink dialog box, as shown in picture 2.7 with the red arrow numbered 1. When you click, a list of web pages appears.

5. **Select** a Web page from the list or **type** the Web page address beside the Address text box to create a hyperlink to a Web page. In our case, we type **http://www.google.com** (shown in picture 2.7 with the red arrow numbered 2).

6. Click the **ScreenTip** button at the top-right corner. It opens the Set Hyperlink ScreenTip dialog box, as shown in picture 2.8.

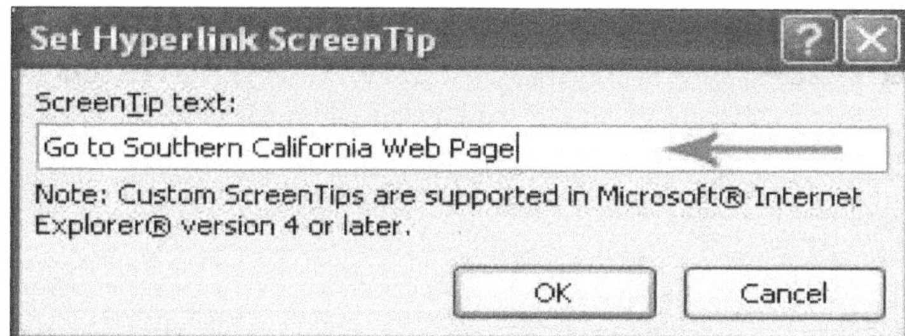

Picture 2.8

7. **Type** a screen tip. In our case, we type: Go to Southern California Web page.

Whenever a user places the mouse-pointer over the hyperlink, a small screen tip appears on the screen. It helps the user to indentify the type of Web page that would appear after clicking the hyperlink.

8. Click the **OK** button in the Set Hyperlink Screen Tip dialog box to close it. The Insert Hyperlink dialog box appears again.

9. Click the **OK** button in the Insert Hyperlink dialog box.

10. **Ctrl+click** the hyperlink (the text you had selected) in your document. As the result, it will open www.google.com Web page. Alternatively, you can right-click a hyperlink and select **Open Hyperlink** from the shortcut menu.

Linking a Document to an Existing Document

In MS Word, you can link a saved Word file in an existing document. Perform the following steps to create a hyperlink to an existing document:

1. **Create** a Word file and save it with the name **Company Info** in My Documents folder.

2. **Close** the Company Info file and **open** a new blank page.

3. **Type** some text in the new page. Then **select** a word or sentence of the new page.

4. Click the **Insert** tab, and click the **Hyperlink** button to open the Insert Hyperlink dialog box.

5. Click the **Current Folder** button in the Insert Hyperlink dialog box. This button is above the Browsed Pages button (already shown in picture 2.7).

6. **Browse** to My Documents folder and select your **Company Info** file.

7. When the Company Info file is selected, click the **OK** button to close the Insert Hyperlink dialog box.

8. **Ctrl+click** the hyperlink (the text you had selected) in the new document. As the result, it will open the **Company Info** file as a hyperlinked file.

Editing and Removing Hyperlinks

You should check the hyperlink in your file from time to time to make sure that they still work. Hyperlinks may get broken when Web pages and parts of files are deleted. Perform the following steps to edit a hyperlink:

1. **Right-click** the hyperlinked text in your document and select **Edit Hyperlink** from the shortcut menu.

The Edit Hyperlink dialog box appears on the screen. This dialog box looks like and works just as the Insert Hyperlink dialog box. You can make changes in the Edit Hyperlink dialog box.

2. **Select** a target file for your document or a Web page.

3. Click the **OK** button at the bottom of the Edit Hyperlink dialog box.

You can also remove a hyperlink that you have created in your document. Perform the following steps to remove a hyperlink:

1. **Right-click** the hyperlinked text in your document.

2. Select the **Remove Hyperlink** from the shortcut menu. As the result, the selected hyperlink is removed from your document.

Creating a Folder

When you work with MS Word in Windows operating system, you may need to create a folder in the hard drive where you can store all your documents. Perform the following steps to create a folder:

1. Click the **Start** button at the bottom-left corner of your monitor screen.

2. Select **My Documents** option from the list.

3. Click **Make a new folder** option which is at the left in the My Documents window.

4. **Enter** the folder name. In our case, we type: **Official**.

5. **Click** outside after you enter the folder name. As the result, a folder named Official is created in the My Documents window.

Alternatively, you can also follow the shortcut to create a folder. For this, first you need to click the **Start** button and select **My Documents**. Then press **right-button** of your mouse in the empty space of the My Documents window, and select **New**. Then select **Folder**, enter the folder's **name**, and click **outside**.

Saving a Word File in Your Folder

By default, MS Word saves your file in My Documents folder. It happens when you click the Save button after clicking the Office Button in Microsoft Word. But if you want to save a file in a particular folder or the folder you have created, you need to select the particular folder at the time of saving the file. Perform the following steps to save a Word file in your Official folder:

1. **Type** some text to create a file in MS Word.

2. Click the **Office Button** at the top-left corner of the MS Word screen.

3. Select the **Save** button from Office Button menu. It displays the <u>Save As</u> dialog box with My Documents folder open, as shown in picture 2.9.

4. Select the folder **Official** from the list in the <u>Save As</u> dialog box, as shown in picture 2.9 with the red arrow.

5. Click the **Open** button at the bottom of the dialog box.

6. **Enter** the file name, and click the **Save** button.

Alternatively, you can also follow this shortcut. Press Ctrl+S to open the Save As dialog box. Then select you folder, click Open button at the bottom, enter the file name, and click the Save button.

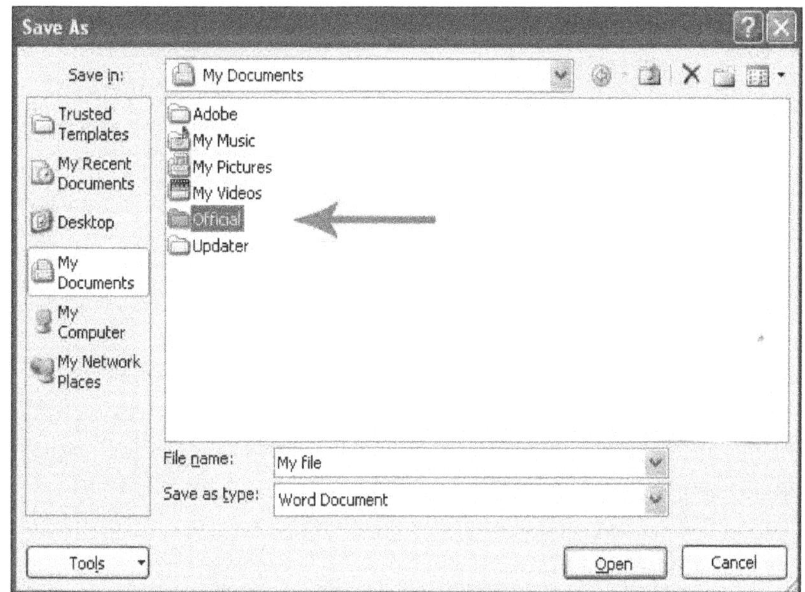

Picture 2.9

Opening a Saved Word File

You can open a saved file to view or edit in MS Word application. MS Word allows you to open your saved Word file in any computer in which this application is installed. Perform the following steps to open a saved word file:

1. Click the **Office Button** at the top-left corner of the MS Word window.

2. Select the **Open** button from Office Button menu. It displays the <u>Open</u> dialog box with My Documents folder open.

3. Select the folder **Official** from the list in the Open dialog box.

4. Click the **Open** button at the bottom of the dialog box.

5. **Select** your file in the list of the Official folder, and click the **Open** button at the bottom of the dialog box.

Alternatively, you can also follow this shortcut. Press Ctrl+O on the keyboard which displays the Open dialog box. Then select your folder, and click the Open button at the bottom. Then select your file, and click the Open button again.

There is one more shortcut to open a saved file. For this, click the Start button on your desktop screen, and select My Documents. Then double-click on your folder to open. After that, double-click on the file that you want to open.

Lesson 5
Learning about Word Processing

Computer typing requires some skill when it comes to accuracy and speed. While typing, you should not look at the keys on the keyboard. You should look at the screen or the sample paper placed at your left hand side. For better typing, the four fingers of your left hand should be placed on the letters A, S, D, F, respectively. And the four fingers of your right hand should be placed on the letters ;, L, K, J, respectively. Both of your thumbs should be placed on the Spacebar. To increase your typing speed, you can type the following sentence at lease fifty times a day:

A quick brown fox jumps over the lazy dog.

This sentence has all the twenty-six letters of the alphabet. Making practice by typing this sentence over and over will help you improve your typing skill. Gradually, you also need to learn the usage of the Spacebar key, Backspace key, Enter key, Shift key, Caps Lock key, four-arrow keys, and the Delete key.

- Spacebar key: Leaves a space where the cursor is blinking.
- Backspace key: Deletes a letter on the left side of the cursor.
- Enter key: Starts a new line.
- Shift key: Types all the letters in upper case when this key is hold down on the keyboard.
- Caps Lock key: When it is pressed once, it types all the letters in upper case.
- Four-arrow keys: Help to move the cursor left, right, up, and down of the text.
- Delete key: Deletes a letter on the right side of the cursor.

Changing the Font Type and Size

A font is a collection of letters, numbers, and symbols in a particular typeface. It includes all italic and boldface variations of the letters, numbers and symbols. Fonts have different names and some of them are many centuries old. Most computers come with different types of fonts, such as Arial, Tahoma, Times New Roman, and Verdana. By default, MS Word often applies the Calibri and Cambria fonts to text.

Selecting Fonts for Text

If you are not satisfied with the default fonts of your text, you can change the fonts. Here are the steps to change the text font:

1. Open a new page by clicking the **Office Button> New> Create** at the bottom-right of the MS Word window. Alternatively, you can press Ctrl+N keys.

2. **Type** some text and **select** it by dragging the screen-pointer while holding the left mouse-button pressed. Alternatively, you can press Ctrl+A keys to select the entire text.

3. Click the **Home** tab at the top of the MS Word window. Then click the **Font** dropdown list under the Font group.

4. Choose **Arial Black** from the Font dropdown list. You can view the live preview of the selected text in the document.

5. **Click** anywhere in the document to remove the highlight. After removing the highlight, the text appears.

You can also change the font type by using some shortcuts mentioned below. These techniques help you change the font type quickly:

- Using Mini Toolbar: Select the text for which you want to change the font. A Mini Toolbar appears beside the selected text on the screen. Then move the mouse-pointer over the Mini Toolbar and select a font in the Font dropdown list.
- Using Shortcut menu: Select the text. Right-click the selected text and select a new font from Mini Toolbar attached to the shortcut menu.
- Using Font dialog box: Select the text. Press Ctrl+D or click the Font group button on the Home tab. It opens the Font dialog box on the screen. Then select a font and click the OK button.

Stylizing the Text

You can make the part of your text bold, italic, or underlined. It helps in drawing the attention of the viewer. To make the text bold, select a part of your text by clicking and dragging the mouse-pointer over it. Then click **B** button in the Font group button on the Home tab.

If you want to make the text italic, select the text and click **I** button in the Font group button on the Home tab. Similarly, to underline your text, click **U** button.

If case you want to make the text normal, you can remove text style. For that, select the stylized part of the text and click **B**, or **I**, or **U** button again. It will remove the applied style from the text you have selected.

Changing the Font Size of Text

All types of font sizes are measured in points. The golden rule of font sizes says that larger the font size, more important is the text. That is why headings are larger than the normal text. Perform the following steps to change the font size of the text:

1. **Select** the text that needs a changed font size. Ensure that the text remains highlighted.

2. Click the **Home** tab at the top, and click the **Font Size** dropdown list.

3. **Move** the mouse-pointer over the font size 16 from the Font Size dropdown list and **click** on it. As the result, the font size of the selected text changes.

4. **Click** anywhere in the document to remove the highlight.

There are some shortcuts to change the font size of the text. For this, select the text and click the Font Size dropdown list. Then type the number (16) from the keyboard, and press the Enter key. Alternatively, you can press Ctrl+Shift+> and Ctrl+Shift+< to increase and decrease the Font Size when the text is selected. For the same effect, you can also use the Grow Font and Shrink Font buttons which are beside the Font Size button in the Font group button on the Home tab.

Creating Headings

MS Word 2013 provides some predefined styles, which ensure how the headings or the text would appear in your document. Styles can greatly improve the appearance and readability of your document. You can make sure that formatting is applied uniformly throughout your document. MS Word makes it easy to apply styles to the selected parts of your documents. On the Home tab, you can see the Styles group. Perform the following steps to apply a style on the text:

1. **Select** the text for which you want to change the style.

2. Click the **Home** tab at the top, and click the dropdown arrow button of the **Styles** group, as shown in picture 3.0 with the red arrow.

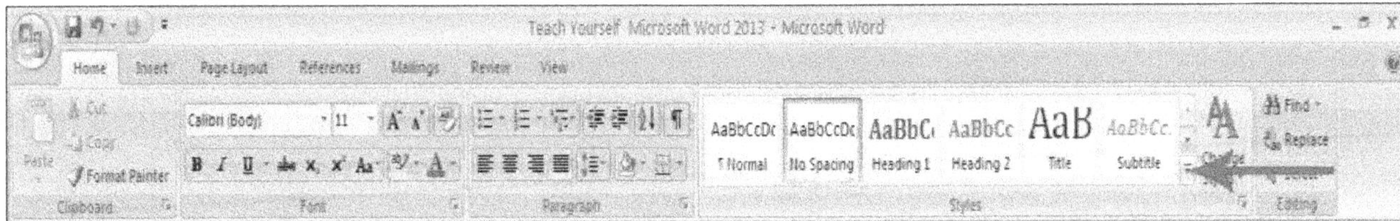

Picture 3.0

3. When the dropdown arrow of the Styles group is clicked, it opens the style list on the screen, as shown in picture 3.1.

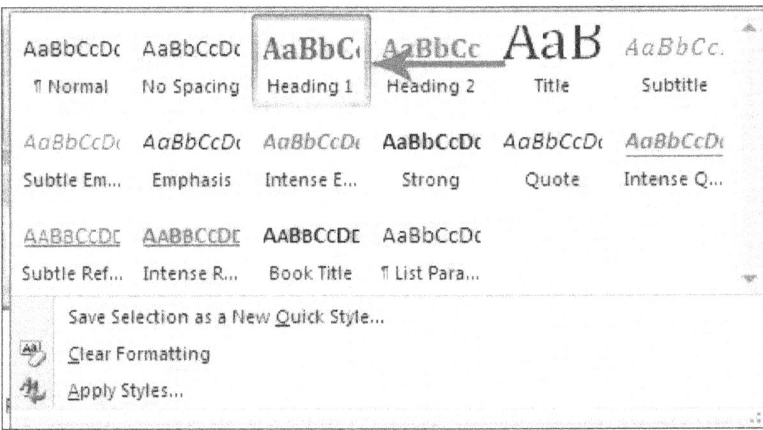

Picture 3.1

4. Click the **Heading 1** style from the style list, as shown in picture 3.1 with the red arrow. As the result, the chosen style is applied on the selected text in the document.

If you want to get a preview of a style, you need to select a portion of your document, and hold mouse over one of the style buttons. You get a quick preview. If you like the style, simply click the button.

Working with a Paragraph

In a word processing program, a paragraph is simply what you put on screen before you press the Enter key. For example, a heading is a paragraph. If you press Enter on a blank line to go to the next line, the blank line is considered a paragraph. If you type Dear Smith at the top of the letter and press Enter, Dear Smith is a paragraph. A paragraph formatting consists of alignment, indentation, and spacing. In a word processing document, paragraph alignment means adjusting the text in a paragraph according to the margins of the document. In indent is the distance between a margin and text, not the edge of the page and text. You can change the indentation of first line as well as entire paragraphs. Spacing is the distance between any two lines in the paragraph. Let's learn how to format a paragraph.

Aligning a Paragraph

The arrangement or position of the text or any object within a document in an organized way is called alignment. MS Word provides four types of alignment – left, right, center, and justify. In a word processing program, text starts out alignment evenly along the left margin, and uneven, or ragged, at the right margin. Left aligned text well for body paragraph in most cases. Other alignments, such as center, right, and justify, change the look of a document. Right-aligned text, which is even along the right margin and ragged at the left margin, is good for adding date to a letter. Justified text spreads evenly between the margins and creates a clean and professional look. Therefore, it is often used in newspapers and magazines. Centered text is best for titles and headings. You can set alignment before or after typing the text by using the alignment buttons on the Home tab. Perform the following steps to learn how to align the text in MS Word:

1. **Select** the paragraph in your text which you want to align.

2. Click the **Home** tab, and click the **Justify** option in the Paragraph group, as shown in picture 3.2 with the red arrow.

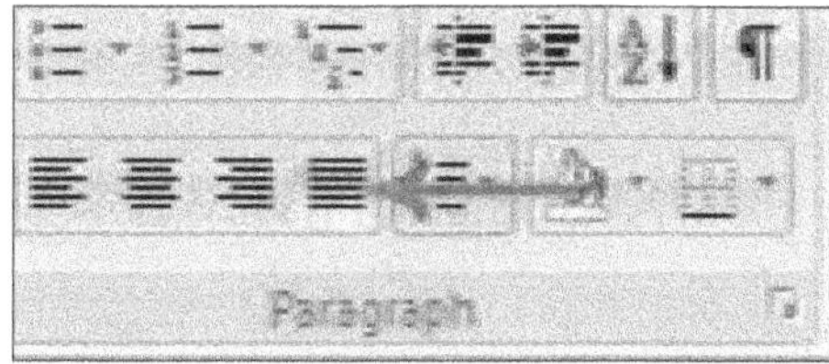

Picture 3.2

As the result, the Justify option aligns the text to both the left and right margins by adding extra space between words as necessary. This creates a clean look along the left and right side of the page.

Working with Paragraph Indentation

Indentation determines the distance of paragraph from either the left or the right margin. Within the margins, you can increase or decrease the indentation of a paragraph or group of paragraphs. You can create a negative indent, also known as outdent, which pulls the paragraph out towards the left margin. In addition, you can create a hanging indent, in which the first line of the paragraph is not indented.

Indenting the First line of a Paragraph

You need to practically learn about indentation in MS Word. Perform the following steps to indent the first line of a paragraph:

1. **Select** a paragraph or group of paragraphs that you want to indent.

2. Click the **Home** tab at the top of the MS Word window.

3. Click the **Paragraph Dialog Box Launcher** button (similar to the launcher button already shown in picture 2.3 with the red arrow). It displays the Paragraph dialog box, in which the **Indent and Spacing** tab appears by default, as shown in picture 3.3.

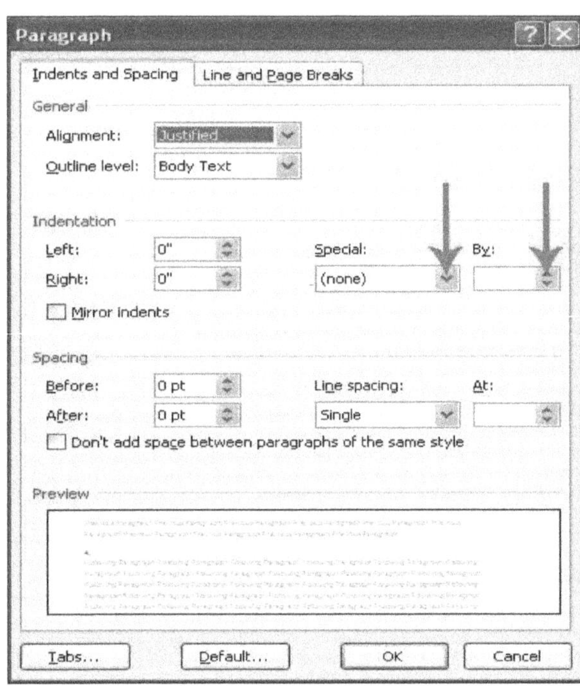

Picture 3.3

4. Click the dropdown button under the **Special** option and select **First line**, as shown in picture 3.3 with the red arrow.

5. **Specify** the value for the first line you want to indent in the By box. In our case, we specify by typing **0.5"**.

The first line of the paragraph that you type would be indented. However, any paragraph before the selected paragraph must be manually indented by using the same procedure.

6. Click the **OK** button at the bottom of the dialog box.

As the result, the first line of the paragraph is indented. Let's now learn to indent left and right margins of a paragraph.

Changing the Left and Right Indent of the Paragraph

MS Word 2013 allows you to increase or decrease the indent of a paragraph. Perform the following steps to increase or decrease the indent of a paragraph:

1. **Select** a paragraph to change its right or left indent.

2. Click **Home** tab, and click the **Paragraph Dialog Box Launcher** button under the Paragraph group. It displays the Paragraph dialog box, in which the Indent and Spacing tab is selected by default.

3. **Click** the up-down arrows next to Left option to increase or decrease the left indentation of the paragraph.

4. **Click** the up-down arrows next to Right option to increase or decrease the right indentation of the paragraph.

5. Click the **OK** button at the bottom of the dialog box. You can also see the preview of Indentation in the Preview area of the Paragraph dialog box.

Working with Spacing in a Paragraph

Spacing affects the readability of a document. Spacing is of two types: line spacing, and paragraph spacing. Line spacing determines the amount of vertical space between the lines of text in a paragraph. If you have long lines of text spanning the width of the page, your eyes have to work to track all the way across it. You should increase the spacing between the lines to follow lines across the page. Paragraph spacing determines the amount of space before and after a paragraph. By default, lines are single spaced, with slightly more space following each paragraph.

Changing the Spacing Before and After Paragraphs

Instead of pressing the Enter key to put a blank line between paragraphs, perform the following steps provide the line spacing before and after a paragraph:

1. **Select** a paragraph or group of paragraphs for which you want to change the spacing.

2. Click **Home** tab, and click the **Paragraph Dialog Box Launcher** button under the Paragraph group. It displays the <u>Paragraph</u> dialog box.

3. Click up or down arrows next to the **Before** option under the <u>Spacing</u> group to increase or decrease the spacing before the paragraph.

4. Click up or down arrows next to the **After** option under the <u>Spacing</u> group to increase or decrease the spacing before the paragraph.

5. Click the **OK** button to close the Paragraph dialog box. As the result, you document appears with the specified changes.

Changing the Line Spacing

If a line contains a large text character, graphic, or formula, MS Word increases the spacing for that line. To space all lines evenly within a paragraph, use exact spacing and specify an amount of space that is large enough to fit the largest character or graphic in the line. If an item appears cut off, increase the amount of spacing. Perform the following steps to change the spacing of a paragraph:

1. **Select** a paragraph for which you want to change the line spacing.

2. Click **Home** tab, and click the **Paragraph Dialog Box Launcher** button under the Paragraph group. It displays the <u>Paragraph</u> dialog box.

3. Click the dropdown button under the **Line spacing** option in the spacing group. A dropdown list of options appears.

4. **Select** an option from the Line spacing dropdown list. In our case, we select **1.5 lines**. Then click the **OK** button at the bottom.

After you leant to change the spacing of a paragraph, now we can discuss about all the options on the list of <u>Line spacing</u> you just saw on your screen:

- **At Least:** Select this option if you want Word to adjust for tall symbols or other unusual text. Word adjusts line spacing according to the value specified in the At Least box.
- **Exactly:** Select this option and enter a number in the **At** box if you want a specific amount of space between lines.
- **Multiple:** Select this option and put a number in the **At** box to get triple-spaced, quadruple, quintuple, or any other number of spaced lines.
- **Single:** Select this option if you want to accommodate the largest font and small amount extra space in a line. The amount of extra space varies depending on the font that is used.
- **1.5 lines:** Select this option if you want to set the spacing one-and-one-half times of single line spacing.

Bulleted and Numbered Lists

You can prepare lists of information in your document by using bullets and numbers. A bulleted list adds bullet dots in front of each list item, while a numbered list adds numbers in front of each list items. A numbered list presents a lot of step-by-step procedures. Bulleted and numbered lists can help you keep your information better organized.

Creating a Bulleted List

Bulleted lists can be used when you want to present alternatives to the reader. A bullet is a black, filled-in circle or other character which you can apply in a document. Perform the following steps to insert bullets to a numbered list:

1. **Select** the text that you want to format.

2. Click the **Home** tab, and click the **Bullets** button under the Paragraph group. As the result, the selected text will appear with bullets on your screen.

Changing the Bullet Style

MS Word allows you to change the bullet style. Perform the following steps on your computer to change the bullet style:

1. **Select** a bulleted list for which you want to change the style of bullets.

2. Click the **Home** tab, and click the dropdown button beside the **Bullets** button under the Paragraph group. It opens a dropdown list on the screen.

3. **Click** a bullet style other than already used. As the result, the new style of bullet is applied to the selected text.

Customizing a Bulleted Style

Creating a customized style or controlling the positioning of bullets can also be done in MS Word. Perform the following steps to create a customized style or control the bullets positioning:

1. **Select** the text that has the bullets applied which you want to customize.

2. **Click** the dropdown button beside the Bullets button. Then click the **Define New Bullet** option from the list to open its dialog box.

3. Click the **Symbol** button in the Define New Bullets dialog box. It opens the Symbol dialog box.

4. Select **Windings** font from the dropdown list beside the Font option in the Symbol dialog box.

5. **Select** a symbol and click the **OK** button at the bottom. The Define New Bullets dialog box reappears.

6. Click the **OK** button again to close the Define New Bullets dialog box.

As the result, you will see the new bullet style applied on the selected text on your screen. The other options in the Define New Bullet dialog box are as follows:

- **Picture:** Opens the Picture Bullet dialog box. In the Picture Bullet dialog box, you can select various colorful bullets and picture bullets for your document.
- **Font:** Allows you to customize the type of font, style, size, and color of the bullet.
- **Alignment:** Specifies the position of the bullet.

Creating a Numbered lists

A numbered list is another way to add emphasis to an item list. In a numbered list, numbers are used to give serial numbers to items. Perform the following steps to create a numbered list:

1. **Select** the item list (text) on which you want to apply numbers.

2. Click the **Home** tab, and click the **Numbering** button under the Paragraph group.

Changing the Numbering Style

If you have applied a numbering style on some text and now you want to change it to some other style, perform the following steps:

1. **Select** the numbered list for which you want to change the numbering style.

2. Click the **Home** tab, and click the dropdown button beside the **Numbering** button under the Paragraph group. It opens a dropdown list.

3. **Click** a number style other than already used. As the result, MS Word applies the new style of numbering to the text selected.

Customizing a Numbering Style

You can create a customized style or control the positioning of numbering. Perform the following steps to create a customized style:

1. **Select** a numbered item list to change its numbering style.

2. Click the **Home** tab, and click the dropdown list button beside the **Numbering** button under the Paragraph group. It opens a dropdown list.

3. Click the **Define New Number Format** option to open its dialog box.

4. Click the dropdown button under the **Number Style** option.

5. **Select** a number style and click the **OK** button to close the Define New Number Format dialog box.

As the result, it creates a customized numbering style. The other options in the Define New Format dialog box are as follows:

- **Font:** Allows you to open the Font dialog box, in which you can customize the type of Font, style, size and color of the numbering.
- **Number Format:** Allows you to customize the predefined number style.
- **Alignment:** Specifies the position of the bullet.

MS Word 2013 applies the customized number style on the selected item list. Besides applying and customizing the lists, there are few tasks related to a list, which are listed as follows:
- **Ending lists:** Allows you to end the list. Right-click the last item in the bulleted list and place mouse-pointer either on Bullets or Numbering option. Another submenu appears. Click the None option.
- **Removing the number, or bullets:** Select the list and click the numbering or bullets button to remove a number or bullet.
- **Adjusting how far a list is indented:** Right-click anywhere in the list, select Adjust List Indents, and enter a new measurement in the Text Indent box.
- **Resuming a numbered list:** Click the Numbering button to start numbering again. The Autocorrect Options button appears. Click it and select Continue Numbering, or right-click and select Continue Numbering on the shortcut menu.
- **Starting a new list:** Suppose that you want to start a brand-new list right away, then Right-click the number and select Restart at 1 on the shortcut menu.

Adding Emphasis to Text and Paragraph

You often want to add special formatting to some text. For example, italics to use in a reference, bold to draw attention to something specific, and some different color of text and highlighting to emphasize text or a paragraph. Let's now learn how to add emphasis to the text and paragraphs.

Making Text Bold, Italic, and Underline

You can use MS Word's basic formatting commands, such as Bold, Italic, and Underline, to quickly add formatting to your text. These three formatting styles are the most common ways to change the appearance of text in a document. You can perform the following steps to apply Bold font style to the text:

1. **Select** the text that you want to make bold.

2. Click the **Home** tab, and click the **Bold** button. This makes the selected text bold in the document.

There are four font styles available in Microsoft Word application. Let's discuss about these font styles in detail:
- **Regular:** Denotes an absence of any font style.
- **Italic:** Emphasis the selected text by making it slightly bent, that is forward inclined.
- **Bold:** Makes the text strong or thick so that it draws attention.
- **Underline:** Draws an underline beneath the text.

You can use the keyboard shortcut (Ctrl+B) to boldface text, (Ctrl+I) to italicize it, or (Ctrl+U) to underline it. To remove a font style, click the Bold, Italic, or Underline button a second time. You can also select text and then click the Clear Formatting button on the Home tab.

Changing the Color of Text and Highlighting the Text

You can add color to the text to enhance the appearance of a document or add emphasis to the text. When selecting text colors, you should not select colors that make your text difficult to read. You can use Word's Highlight tool to add highlighting to the text in a document. For example, if you share a document with others, you can highlight a sentence or paragraph that you add to the document to draw attention to the new addition. You might also highlight the text that you want a colleague to check. When you apply highlighting, you can specify a highlight color. Perform the following steps to change the color of the text:

1. **Select** the text that you want to format.

2. Click the **Home** tab, and click the **Font Color** button. It opens a dropdown list.

3. **Click** a color to select it.

You can also select More Colors in Font Color box. Then select your color under Standard tab or create your color under Custom tab. By the way, you can also select one these techniques to change the color of the text:

- Open the dropdown list on the Font Color buttons and select a color from the Mini Toolbar.
- Right-click the selected text to opens a dropdown list. Then click the Font Color option and select a color in the Fonts dialog that appears.
- Click the Font group button to open the Font dialog box, open the Font Color dropdown list, and select a color.

The Font Color dropdown list offers theme and standard colors. You are well advised to select a theme color. Theme colors are referred to those colors, which live with the theme you select for your file. Perform the following steps to highlight the text:

1. **Select** the text that you want to highlight.

2. Click the **Home** tab, and click the **Text Highlight Color** button.

3. **Choose** a color and **click** outside. As the result, the text is highlighted.

If you want to remove the Text Highlight Color, first you need to **select** the highlighted text, and then click the dropdown button of **Text Highlight Color**, and then choose **No Color** and click outside.

Using Clear Formatting

You can use Clear Formatting option in MS Word to remove all the effects and styles applied to the text. Perform the following steps to remove text formatting:

1. **Select** the text on which you have applied formatting. You can press Ctrl+A to select the entire text of the document.

2. Click the **Home** tab, and click the **Clear Formatting** button in Font group. This button is just above the Font Color button. It will remove all effects as well as bullets and numbering from the text.

Lesson 6
Editing Techniques
In Microsoft Word, you can use many techniques to do things quickly and efficiently. There are shortcuts of several commands which save your time while typing. Some of these shortcuts are used in all Microsoft applications and other software also.

Cut and Paste
While typing, at several times you need to delete a word or sentence from one place and paste it another place. If you go the conventional way of deleting a particular word and retyping it at some other place, it is going to take more time. For this, you can use the Cut and Paste command to delete the part of a text from one place, and paste it at another place. Perform the following steps to use the Cut and Paste command:

1. **Select** a word or sentence from a text.

2. In the <u>Home</u> tab, click the **Cut** button which is in the <u>Clipboard</u> group just below the Home tab. It deletes the selected word and saves in the Clipboard.

3. **Move** the cursor to a new location.

4. Click the **Paste** button which is in the Clipboard group in Home tab. It pastes the selected word at the new location.

You may prefer to use keyboard shortcuts for the Cut and Paste command. For this, Ctrl+A allows you to cut the selected text, and Ctrl+V allows you to paste the text.

Copy and Paste
Using the Copy and Paste command, you can make a copy of the selected word and paste it at different locations as many times you want. Perform the following steps to use the Copy and Paste command:

1. **Select** a word or sentence from a text.

2. In the <u>Home</u> tab, click the **Copy** button which is in the <u>Clipboard</u> group. You can use the shortcut Ctrl+V for this.

3. **Move** the cursor to a new location.

4. Click the **Paste** button in the Clipboard group. It pastes the selected word at the new location. You can paste this word as many times you want.

Moving the Text
MS Word allows you to move the selected text from one place to another. It saves your time of cutting and pasting the text. You can easily move the text using the mouse-pointer. Perform the following steps to move the text:

1. **Select** a word or sentence from a text.

2. **Place** the mouse-pointer on (in the middle) of the selected text.

3. **Press** and **hold** the left mouse-button.

4. **Drag-and-drop** the selected word to any location you want.

Using Strikethrough

The Strikethrough button draws a line through the middle of the selected word. After you click this button, it makes the selected word or sentence looks like you have wronged it. You may need this command in your document editing. Perform the following steps to use the Strikethrough command:

1. **Select** a word or sentence from a text.

2. Click the **Strikethrough** button in the Home tab. This button is beside the Underline button in the Font group.

As the result, it draws a line through the middle of the selected word. Like this, you can also use the Subscript, Superscript, and Change Case buttons to see the effects on the selected text.

Using Format Painter

Format Painter is a magnificent tool in MS Word. Using this tool, you can apply the formatting style of one text onto another text without using copy-and-paste command. Perform the following simple steps for this:

1. **Type** two sentences in your MS Word page.

2. **Select** the first sentence and **change** its font style to Arial Black.

3. **Select** the first sentence, and click the **Format Painter** button in the Clipboard group of the Home tab.

4. **Drag** the mouse-pointer on the second sentence in the page. As the result, it applies the font style (Arial Black) of first sentence to the second sentence.

Undo and Redo

You need to use this command several times in typing and editing a document. In MS Word, the Undo command takes you one step back from where you are. And the Redo command puts you to the same place where you undid. Perform the following steps to do it practically:

1. **Type** a word and **apply** red color on it.

2. Click the **Undo** button which is at the top-left corner of the MS Word window. You may like to use the shortcut **Ctrl+Z** for this. It removes the red color from the word.

3. Click the **Redo** button or press the **Ctrl+Y** shortcut. It brings the red color back on the word.

If you click the small dropdown button beside the Undo button at the top-left corner of the MS Word screen, you can undo several steps at a time.

Working with WordArt

WordArt is a predefined design of the decorative text that you can insert in a document. After inserting a WordArt, you can change its size, color, orientation, and shape. You can also apply shadow and 3D effects on the WordArt. It makes the document attractive and gives the impression as if the art is designed in the desktop publishing software, such as CorelDraw or Photoshop. Perform the following steps to insert a WordArt:

1. Click the **Insert** tab at the top of the MS Word window.

2. Click the **WordArt** button which is in the Text group in the Insert tab, as shown in picture 3.4 with the red arrow. It opens a list of designs on the screen.

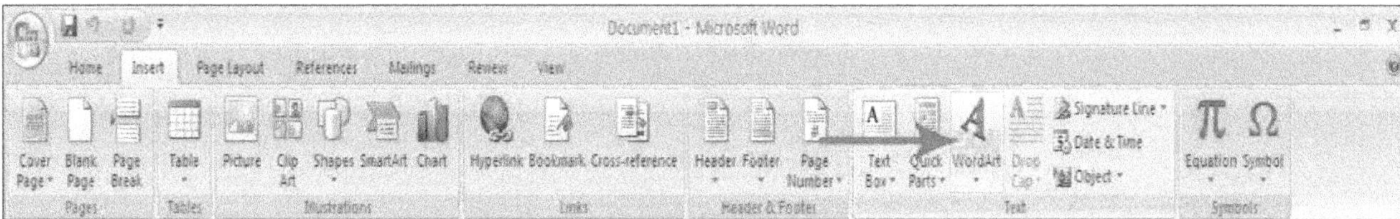

Picture 3.4

3. In the list of designs (shown in picture 3.5), **select** a design. It opens the Edit WordArt Text dialog box.

4. **Type** a word in the Edit WordArt Text dialog box, and click the **OK** button at the bottom. In our case we type the word: Cromosys.

As the result, the WordArt is inserted in the document, as shown in picture 3.6. It appears with handles (buttons) on all the sides of the WordArt. If you drag any handle with your mouse-pointer, you will be able to enlarge or shorten the WordArt.

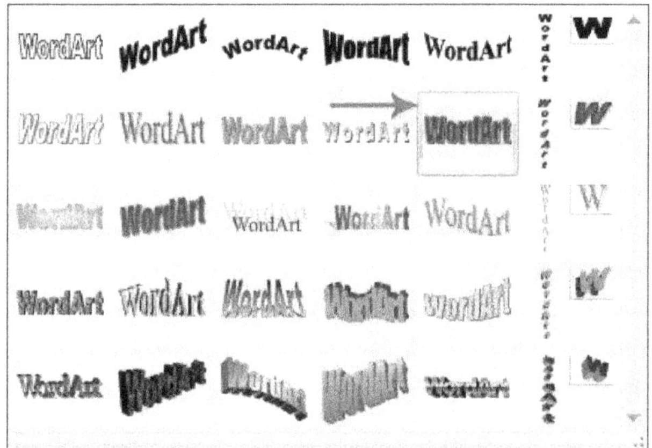

Picture 3.5

Picture 3.6

Editing the WordArt

Editing of the WordArt involves moving, changing rotation and orientation, and filling color in the WordArt. When you insert a WordArt in a document, it appears with a dotted line all around the WordArt, as shown in picture 3.6. This line is technically called a wrapping-line. Until the WordArt is inside the wrapping-line, you cannot move the WordArt in the document. Therefore, you need to remove the wrapping-line first, and then move ahead with editing the WordArt. Perform the following steps to edit the WordArt starting with removing the wrapping-line:

1. **Select** the WordArt by clicking on it.

2. Click the **Format** tab at the top of the MS Word screen. This tab appears only when you select the WordArt.

3. Click the **Text Wrapping** dropdown button which is towards the right side in the Ribbon. It opens a dropdown list.

4. **Click** on any option in the dropdown list. As the result, it will remove the wrapping-line from the WordArt.

5. As the WordArt is still selected, **left-click** the WordArt and **drag and drop** it anywhere in the page. This way, you can move the WordArt anywhere in the document.

6. Click the **green button** at the top of the WordArt, and **rotate** it the way you want. Then click the **yellow button** at the left side of the WordArt, and **change** its orientation.

Filling Color in the WordArt

MS Word allows you to change the color of the WordArt. Perform the following steps to fill a color in the WordArt:

1. **Select** the WordArt and click the **Format** tab at the top.

2. Click the **Shape Fill** dropdown button which is just below the Format tab.

3. **Choose** any color from the dropdown. It changes the color of the WordArt.

4. Keeping the WordArt selected, you can click the **Shape Outline** dropdown button In the Format tab.

5. **Choose** any color from the dropdown. It changes the outline color of the WordArt.

6. Click the **Change Shape** dropdown button which is below the Shape Outline button in the Format tab.

7. **Select** any shape from the dropdown list. It changes the shape of the WordArt.

8. In the <u>WordArt Styles</u> group under Format tab, click the **up-down arrow** button to scroll the style list.

9. **Choose** any style from the list. In our case, we choose **WordArt style 16**.

Applying WordArt Shadow and 3D

MS Word allows you to apply shadow and 3D style to the WordArt. This effect makes the WordArt alluring and looks beautiful when you print the WordArt. Perform the following steps for this:

1. **Select** the WordArt and click the **Shadow Effects** dropdown button in the Format tab.

2. **Select** any style from the dropdown list. In our case, we select the Shadow style 20 which is at the bottom of the list, as shown in picture 3.7.

Picture 3.7

3. Click the **Shadow Effects** button, and click the **Shadow Color** option at the bottom

4. **Choose** any color from the list of colors. It will change the shadow color of the WordArt.

5. Click on any of the **four-arrow buttons** beside the Shadow Effects button. It will rotate the shadow of the WordArt you have applied.

6. **Select** the WordArt and click the **3D Effects** dropdown button in Format tab. Then **choose** any style from the list.

7. Click the **3D Effects** button, click the **3D Color** option at the bottom, and **choose** any 3D color.

8. Click on any of the **four-arrow buttons** beside the 3D Effects button. It will rotate the 3D effect of the WordArt. You can also use Depth, Direction, Lighting, and Surface options under 3D Effects button.

Adding Borders and Shading to a Paragraph

After learning about WordArt, now you can learn to add borders to your document text. It adds emphasis or makes the document more appealing. For instance, you can add a border to a paragraph to bring attention to the text. You can also add a border to the entire document page. Adding border to an important paragraph helps it stand out from the rest of your document. Perform these steps to add a border and shading to a paragraph:

1. **Select** a paragraph to which you want to add border and shading.

2. Click the **Home** tab, and click the **Border** button which is in the Paragraph group.

3. Select the **Borders and Shading** option at the bottom. It displays a dialog box which is shown in picture 3.8.

4. Click the **Box** option on the left side in the Border and Shading dialog box, as shown in picture 3.8 with the red arrow numbered 1.

5. **Scroll** through the Style list to select a Border design, as shown in picture 3.8 with the red arrow numbered 2. You can also select a custom color and width. There is a small preview window on the right side of the dialog box.

6. Click the **Shading** tab, as shown in picture 3.8 with the red arrow numbered 3. By the way, adding too many effects to the document can make the document difficult to read.

7. **Click** the dropdown arrow under the **Fill** option and **select** the color of your choice. You can also click the Style dropdown list to add the intensity to the color.

8. Click the **OK** button to close the Borders and Shading dialog box. You can see the effect applied to the text on your screen.

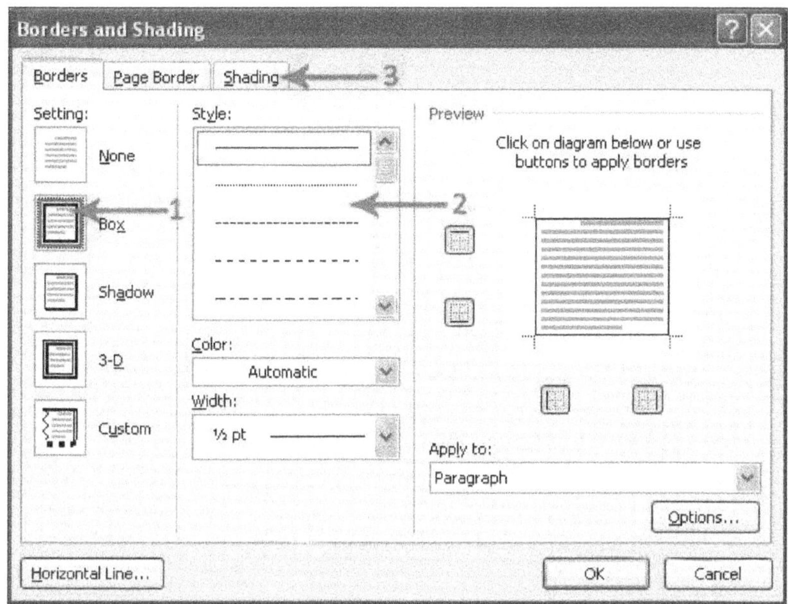

Picture 3.8

Inserting a Table

A table is a grid of cells with individual cells occurring at the intersection of corresponding rows and columns. Tables are highly customizable and useful for a variety of tasks ranging from presenting numerical data to creating unique layouts. You can use tables to present data in an organized fashion. For example, you can add a table to your document to display a list of items or present data in a category.

Setting Rows and Columns

Tables are built with columns and rows that intersect to form cells. You can insert all types of data, including text and graphics, in table cells. Perform the following steps to insert a table in a document:

1. **Click** at the point where you want to insert a table in your document.

2. Click the **Insert** tab, and click the **Table** button.

3. Click the **Insert Table** option to open its dialog box. The Insert Table dialog box is shown in picture 3.9.

4. **Type 4** beside the Number of columns option, and **type 4** beside the Number of rows option in the Insert Table dialog box.

5. Click the **OK** button to close the Insert Table dialog box. As the result, a table with four columns and rows is inserted in the document (shown in picture 4.0).

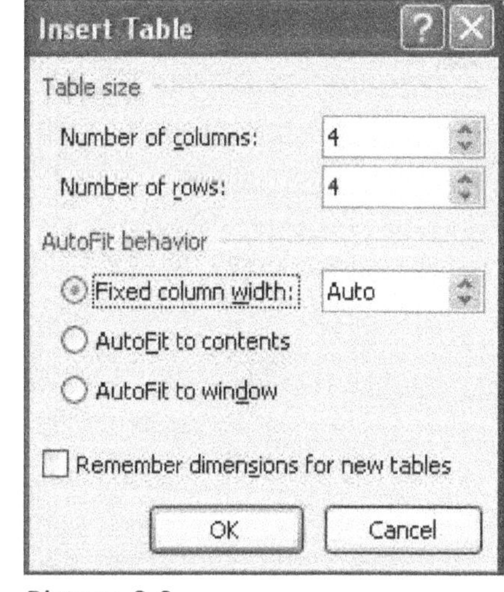

Picture 3.9

Item Sales Report			

Picture 4.0

If you find this way difficult to insert a table, there are other simple ways for it. Perform the following steps to create a table from the table dropdown list:

1. Click the **Table** button present in the <u>Insert</u> tab. It opens a dropdown list on the screen.

2. **Select** the number of <u>columns</u> and <u>rows</u> from the dropdown list.

3. **Click** the place where you want to insert the table. The preview of the rows and columns are viewed directly on the table.

The table will appear on the page where your cursor is blinking. You can move the cursor to different columns using the **Tab key** on the keyboard. Don't press the Enter key.

Creating a Quick Table

You can also create a quick table by selecting a predefined table from the submenu. Perform the following steps to create a quick table:

1. Click the **Table** button present in the Insert tab.

2. Select **Quick Tables** in the dropdown list.

3. **Select** a predefined table from the submenu.

After creating a table, you get two new tabs on Ribbon. The ribbon is the bar with options at the top of the MS Word screen. The Design tab (for tables) offers commands to change the look of the table. The Layout tab (for tables) is used to change the rows and columns.

Adding Information to the Table

A newly created table contains no information by default. In order to make table meaningful, you need to insert data on your own in each cell of the table. You can start entering data by clicking a cell and start typing. Perform the following steps to add information to the table:

1. **Click** inside the first cell of the table and **type** Item Name.

2. Press the **Tab key** from the keyboard after writing the text in the first column. Using Tab key, you can move the cursor from one column to another and from one row to another.

Inserting Rows and Columns

Sometimes you need to expand your existing table to accommodate more details. For that, you have to insert rows and columns in a table. You can insert new row before or after an existing row or at the end of the table. Perform the following steps to insert a new row after the last row of the table:

1. **Move** the mouse-pointer at the last row of the first column.

2. Click the **Layout tab** (for tables) at the top of the MS Word window.

3. Click the **Insert below** button under the Rows & Columns group. As the result, a row is inserted in the table at the end.

You can also add a new column in a table. The new column would be placed to the left or right side of an existing column or after the last column in the table. Perform the following steps to add a new column between two existing columns in the table:

1. **Move** the mouse-pointer at the first column and in the first row.

2. Click the **Layout tab** (for tables) at the top.

3. Click the **Insert Right** button under the Rows & Columns group. As the result, a column is inserted between the existing columns in the table.

Deleting Rows and Columns

You may need to delete one or more rows or column from your table. You can do this in the following ways:

1. **Click** in the column or rows you want to delete.

2. Click the **Delete** button on the Layout tab. It opens a dropdown list on the screen.

3. Click the **Delete Columns** (or rows) option from the dropdown list.

You can delete more than one column or rows if you want. For that, you need to select more than one column or rows. Not that pressing the Delete key on the keyboard deletes the data in the column, not the column itself.

Deleting the entire Table

You can delete the entire table along with the data from the document. Here are the steps to delete the entire table:

1. **Click** in any cell in the table.

2. Click the **Delete** button on the Layout tab.

3. Click the **Delete Table** option from the dropdown list.

Saving the Document

The document created by you is temporary till the time it is not assigned a name and saved at an appropriate location on your computer for future references. After saving the document, you can reuse and share it with your friends. In this section, we would learn to save the document in its default mode (that is with DOCX extension) as well as in compatibility mode (that is with DOC extension) so that users who do not have the latest version of MS Office could open and edit the document.

Saving a Document in DOCX Extension

You can save your data to reuse or share it with others. You should also frequently save any file that you are working on to prevent data lose in case of a power failure or computer crash. When you save a file, you can give it a unique filename, and store it in a particular folder or drive. Perform the following steps to save the file:

1. Click **Office Button** at the top of the MS Word window.

2. Click the **Save As** button in the dropdown list. It opens the Save As dialog box on the screen.

You can also click the Save button on the Quick Access toolbar to save the document for the first time. In case the document is already saved, then you can use the Save button on the Quick Access toolbar to frequently save changes carried out in the document.

3. Click the **Navigation pane** on the left of the Save As dialog box to navigate the folder in which you want to save the file.

4. **Type** the file name beside the File name option. Then click the **Save** button at the bottom of the dialog box. It will close the Save As dialog box.

Saving the Document in Compatibility Mode

The users who do not have at least MS Word 2007 installed on their computers, they can not open the Word file created in the DOCX format. Therefore, before you pass to some other person who has an older version of MS Office, you need to save your document in the formats used by such versions. Perform the following simple steps to save a file in a format that can be opened in Office 97, 2000, XP, or 2003.

1. Click **Office Button** at the top of the MS Word window.

2. **Move** the mouse-pointer to the dropdown arrow beside the Save As option. It opens a list of options on the right side.

3. Click the **Word 97-2003 Document** option. It opens the Save As dialog box.

4. **Type** a new file name beside the File name text box.

5. **Select** the location in the **Navigation** pane. Then click the **Save** button to save the file in the 97-2003 format with a DOC file extension.

Printing the Document

Email and Web documents are bringing the paperless office closer to reality. However, the most common way to distribute a finished document is still to print it. As a result of advancements in printing technology, it is now possible to print on both sides of the paper. Such a technique is known as duplex printing. If you have latest printer, then you can perform duplex printing from MS Word 2013 to give more professional look to your printed document. Let's learn to preview the document and apply some settings before printing.

Getting a Print Preview of the Document

Although creating documents in Word is great, there are times when you want to print a paper copy. Before you print the document; however, you should make sure that everything is fine and as per your requirement. Perform the following steps to preview a document:

1. **Open** the document that you want to print.

2. Click **Office Button** and move the mouse-pointer over the dropdown arrow beside the **Print** option.

3. Click the **Print Preview** option. As the result, it will show the document on the screen as it would be printed.

When you click the Print Preview option, the default ribbons disappear from the screen. The Print Preview tab appears at the top. The Print Preview tab provides various options to view your document differently. Let's now discuss various categories available in the Print Preview tab:

Print Preview Tab Options

Group	Options	Description
Print	Print	Opens the Print dialog box.
	Options	Opens the Display section of the Word Options dialog box.
Page Setup	Margins	Changes the white space around the edge of the page.
	Orientation	Changes the layout of the document.
	Size	Changes the size of the page.
	Option button	Opens the Page Setup dialog box.
Zoom	Zoom	Opens the Zoom dialog box.
	100%	Returns to default zoom level.
	One Page	Refers to the option that is used to view one page.
	Two Pages	Allows you to view two pages.
	Page Width	Allows you to view page width.
Preview	Show Ruler	Shows you the ruler.
	Magnifier	Turns your cursor into a magnifying glass. You can click to zoom in and click again to zoom out.
	Shrink One Page	Shrinks the document to one page.
	Next Page	Goes to the next page.
	Previous Page	Goes to the Previous page.
	Close Print Preview	Closes the Print Preview window.

Setting Printing Options

Printing options can be set from the Print dialog box. You can give the print command to print a document. Click the Print button on the Print Preview tab to open the Print dialog box. The Print dialog box appears on your screen, as shown in picture 4.0.

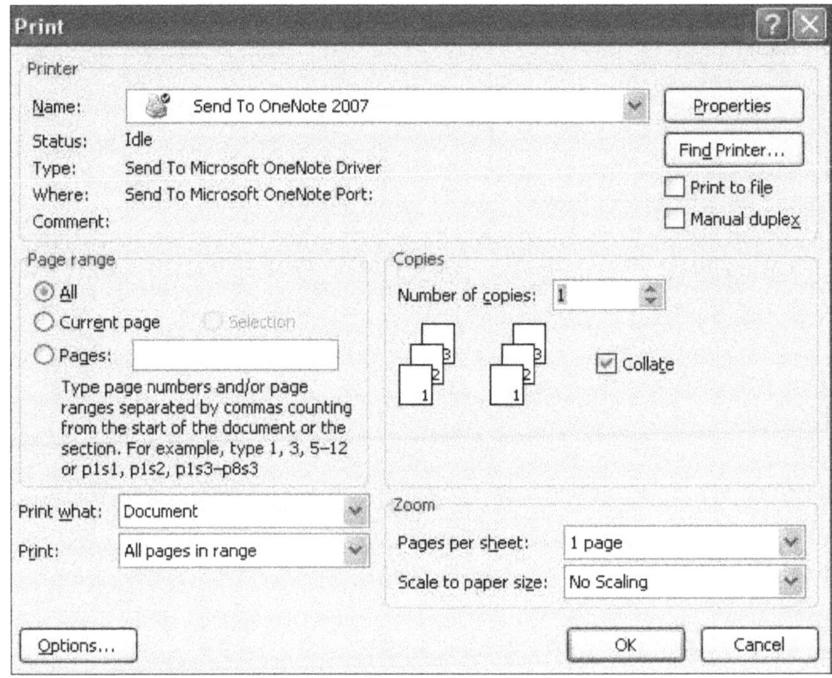

Picture 4.0

The Print dialog box offers the following setting options:

- **Printer:** Allows you to select a printer to print the document.
- **Page Range:** Allows you to specify range of pages for printing. In this option, you can select to print all pages, the current page, or just a selection. You can also click the Pages radio button and enter page numbers. You can specify pages in a number of ways. Suppose a document contains 20 pages, then we can use the page ranges in the ways given in the table below:

The Information about Page Ranges

Page Range Values	Output Generated by the Printer
1,3,5	Out of 20 page document, printer prints only pages one, three, and five.
1-5	Out of 20 page document, printer prints pages one to five only.
-5	Out of 20 page document, printer prints only first five pages of the document.
5-	Out of 20 pages, printer prints page five onwards (till the end of the document).
3	Out of 20 page document, printer prints only page 3.
1,3,5,9-11,17	Out of 20 page document, printer prints page one, three and five; pages nine to eleven; and page seventeen.

- **Copies:** Allows you to specify number of copies of printout. By default one copy of entire document or specified page range is printed. You can increase the number of copies for printing by clicking up-arrow button beside the Copies option or double-click the text box to highlight the value and then type new value to specify number of copies for printout.

Closing the Document

After working on a document and saving it, you can close the document. Perform the following steps to close the document:

1. Click **Office Button** to open its dropdown list.

2. Click the **Close** button in the list. MS Word 2013 closes the document.

3. You can exit from the MS Word application by clicking the **Exit Word** button on the Office Button dropdown list.

Lesson 7
Tools and Options

You will rarely write a document that does not require editing. You will almost always want to insert a word or two, change a phrase, or move text from one place to another. You can edit a document as you create it, or you can write it first and the revise it. At times, you may want to edit a document that you created for one purpose to make it serve a different purpose. For example, a document from the last year's marketing campaign might be edited to create a new letter for this year's campaign. In the days of handwritten and typewritten documents, people might have tolerated a spelling or grammar error because correcting these types of errors was very difficult. However, documents that contain errors create a bad impression about their writers. Although, MS Word has in-built spelling and grammar checkers that help you to eliminate misspelled words and grammatical errors. In MS Word, you can track each insertion, deletion, formatting change, or comment that you make in the document so that you can review these modifications later. In this lesson, you learn to find and replace text and check spelling and grammatical errors in a document. You also learn to translate a document in foreign languages.

Finding and Replacing Text

It is a very difficult and tedious task to find a word in a large document. The most common technique to navigate a large document is the Find command, which locates all instances of a word or phrase in the document. MS Word also provides you the Replace command together with the Find command to change a word, phrase, or text throughout the document. For example, suppose that your company has changed its name. If you want to change the old company name in an official document, then you can use the Replace command to replace all the instances of old company name with the new name in a very less time. Let's now learn how Find and Replace commands work in a document.

Find Instances of Specific Text in the Document

In a Word document, you can quickly and easily search for every occurrence of a specific word or phrase. Perform the following steps to find all instances of specific text in a document:

1. Click the **Home** tab at the top of the MS Word window.

2. Click the **Find** button (Ctrl+F) in the Editing group. It opens the **Find and Replace** dialog box on the screen.

3. **Type** a word which you want to search in the <u>Find what</u> text box. In our case, we have typed **Games** in the Find what text box.

4. Click the **Find Next** button in the dialog box.

Microsoft Word starts searching all the instances of text (Games) in the document. When it finds the first instance of word Games, it highlights the word in the document. You can keep on clicking the **Find Next** button to find more instances of word Games in the document.

5. Click the **Cancel** button to stop finding more instances of text in the document.

Features of the Search Options

The Find and Replace dialog box is closed when you click the Cancel button. At times, you may realize that you need to run the same search again. Instead of opening the Find and Replace dialog box again, you can repeat the most recent search by pressing the Shift+F4 keys. The Find and Replace dialog box contains various search options that help you to refine your search. You can take control of your search by utilizing the features of the **Search Options** group. Perform the following steps to use the Search Options group:

1. Click the **Home** tab, and click the **Find** button in the <u>Editing</u> group.

2. **Type** a word which you want to search in the <u>Find what</u> text box. In our case, we type **Games**.

3. Click the **More** button at the bottom-left corner in the Find and Replace dialog box. The **Search Options** group appears in the Find and Replace dialog box, as shown in picture 4.1.

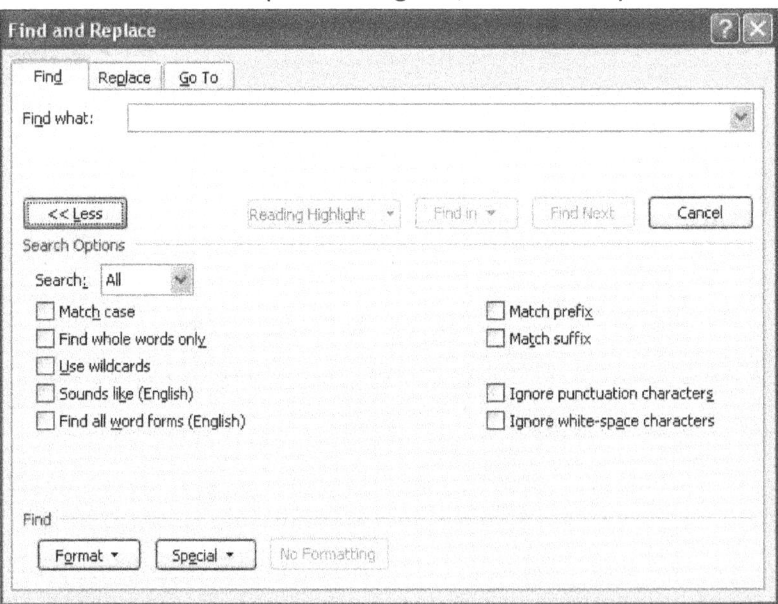

Picture 4.1

After learning to open the Search Options group, let's now discuss the features of this group that can be used to improve your search:

- **Search:** Allows you to specify a direction for MS Word to search the instances of text mentioned by the user. The default direction to search instances of text is **All**, which searches the entire document (down to the end and then continuing from the beginning). You can also click either Down (towards the end of the document) or Up (towards the start). If you are sure the instance is later or earlier in the document, specifying a direction can speed up the search because Word does not have to go through the entire file.
- **Match case:** Allows you to find only those instances that match the uppercase and lowercase letters, which you have specified in the Find what text box. For example, if you type **Book** as the search text, Find will match Book but not *book* or *BOOK*.
- **Find whole words only:** Allows you to find only those instances of the search text that are entire words, not just partial words. For example, if you type **pen** as the search text, you can only get the word pen, not the words that contains *-pen-,* such as *expenses* and *pencil*.
- **Use wildcards:** Allows you to use wildcard characters in your search text. Wildcard characters enable you to search the text of a specific pattern.
- **Sounds like (English):** Allows you to match words that are same phonetically as the search text. For example, if you type **color** in the Find what text box; this option also matches the variant spelling **colour** and works for phonetic matches, such as *bold* and *bowled* and *mail* and *male*.
- **Find all word forms (English):** Allows you to match all the verb forms of the search text. For example, if you type **sink** in the Find what text box, you get only **sink**, but also *sinking*, *sank*, and *sunk*.
- **Match prefix:** Allows you to match words that begin with the search text. For example, if you type **hyper** in the Find what text box, you get all the words with hyper prefix, such as *hyperlink* and *hyperactive* (also the word hyper).
- **Match suffix:** Allows you to match words that end with the text entered in the Find what text box. For example, if you type **space** in the Find what text box, you get all the words with space suffix, such as *monospace* and *cyberspace* (also the word space).
- **Ignore punctuation characters:** Allows you to bypass punctuation marks while searching for text or phrase in the document. For example, if you type **well** in the Find what text box, you get *we'll* and *we;ll*.
- **Ignore while-space characters:** Allows you to bypass white spaces while searching for text or phrase in the document. For example, if you specify a whitespace (space and tabs) in the Find what text box, Find command will look for the matching whitespace but if you select **Ignore white-space characters** check box, Find command will ignore spaces and tabs.

Replace Text with Another Text

If you have a number of instances of a word or phrase that require the same edit, you can use the Replace command, which saves a lot of your valuable time and makes the editing easier. Perform the following steps to execute the Replace operation in a document:

1. Click the **Home** tab, and click the **Replace** button (Ctrl+H) in the <u>Editing</u> group.

2. **Type** the word or phrase that you want to edit in the <u>Find what</u> text box. In our case, we type the word **machine**.

3. **Type** the text which you want to use as the replacement in the <u>Replace with</u> text box. In our case, we type **device**.

4. Click the **Find Next** button in the Find and Replace dialog box. As the result, MS Word selects the next instance of the text.

5. Click the **Replace** button in the same dialog box.

Keep on clicking the Replace button to continue replacing the text. If you come across an instance where you do not want to replace, *click* the **Find Next** button. If you want to replace all instances of the text, select the Replace All option. After replacing all instances of the text in the document, the Cancel button transforms into the Close button. Click the Close button to close down the Find and Replace dialog box.

6. Click the **Cancel** button if you wish to discontinue replacing the text.

Using the Go To Command

If you have a document of many pages, and you need to reach a particular page in a quick span of time, you can use the Go To command. Using this command you can directly reach the particular page without scrolling the pages or using the Page Up or Page Down keys on the keyboard. Perform the following steps to use the Go To command:

1. **Open** a document in MS Word which has many pages.

2. Click the **Home** tab, and click the **Find** button. It opens the Find and Replace dialog box.

3. Click the **Go To** tab in the Find and Replace dialog box. Alternatively, you can directly press **Ctrl+G** shortcut keys to reach the Go To section.

4. **Enter** the page number in the Enter page number text box. In our case, we enter **10**.

5. Click the **Go To** button at the bottom of the Find and Replace dialog box. As the result, it will directly take you to the page.

Checking Spelling and Grammar Mistakes

As you type text in a Word document, the spell checker operates in the background and examines spelling errors in the text. MS Word indicates the spelling errors with a red wavy line under that word. No matter how professionally organized and formatted your document appears; a simple spelling error can take a reader's mind off your document. However, mistakes can occur especially in large documents. You can overcome the problems of spelling errors by using the spell-check feature of MS Word. This spell-check feature identifies spelling errors, explains what the errors are, and gives you the alternatives and opportunities to correct the errors. Perform the following steps to correct a misspelled word:

1. **Right-click** the misspelled word which is indicated with a red wavy line in the document. It opens a shortcut menu.

2. **Click** the correct replacement of misspelled word in the shortcut menu. As the result, the correct word replaces the misspelled word in the document.

At the time of correcting misspelled words, you must have noticed some options in the shortcut menu. The functions of these options are as follows:

- **Correction:** Allows you to click one of those suggestions that are provided by the spell checker to correct the word.
- **Ignore:** Allows you to leave the word as it is and does not perform any spell check on it. For example, it might be a company name or code word written uniquely; therefore spell checker is showing error. In that case, you can ignore the suggestions provided by the spell checker.
- **Ignore All:** Allows you to remove the red underline from all instances of the word in the current document. However, if you restart Word, it will again flag this word as an error.
- **Add to Dictionary:** Allows you to insert a term into dictionary. If a word is spelled correctly and you do not want Word to flag it again, you can add that word into the Word dictionary.
- **Auto Correct:** Allows you to correct an error that you usually make. When you click this option, it provides you a list of suggestions. You can click the desired suggestion to select it. Next time when you misspell the word, Word will automatically correct it.
- **Spelling:** Allows you to open the Spelling and Grammar dialog box.

The grammar checker also operates in the background and searches your text for grammatical errors. If you make any grammar error, the grammar checker shows you a green wavy line under the sentence or word. Perform the following steps to correct a grammatical error:

1. **Right-click** the green-underlined text.

2. **Click** the correct replacement in the shortcut menu. As the result, the MS Word replaces the grammar mistake.

At the time of correcting grammatical errors in the document, you must have noticed some options in the shortcut menu. The functions of these options are as follows:

- **Corrections:** Allows you to click one of the suggestions provided by the grammar checker to correct the text.
- **Ignore Once:** Allows you to bypass the current instance of error in the current document.
- **Grammar:** Allows you to open the Spelling and Grammar dialog box.
- **About this sentence:** Allows you to display the Word Help dialog box, which explains the error and offers suggestions to avoid the error in future.

Correcting Spelling and Grammar Mistakes

You can correct the misspelled words by running the spell check in your document. You can also invoke the grammar checker along with the spell-checker. Before launching the spell checker, first decide what you want to check. If you want to check just a word or a section of text, select the text; if you want to check the entire document, move the cursor to the top of the file and perform the following steps to correct the spelling and grammar mistakes in the document:

1. Click the **Review** tab at the top of the MS Word screen.

2. Click the **Spelling and Grammar** button in the Proofing group.

The **Spelling and Grammar: English (U.S.)** dialog box appears on the screen, as shown in picture 4.2. If the spell checker does not find any error, it displays a message box to let you know that the check is complete. Otherwise, it displays the **Spelling and Grammar: English (U.S.)** dialog box. In the **Not in Dictionary** box, the misspelled word is highlighted, whereas, in the **Suggestions** box correct words are displayed. For example, the misspelled word executable appears highlighted in the Not in Dictionary box where as correct words with closest possible meaning of misspelled word appears in the Suggestion box. In the **Suggestions** box, the correct spelling is shown.

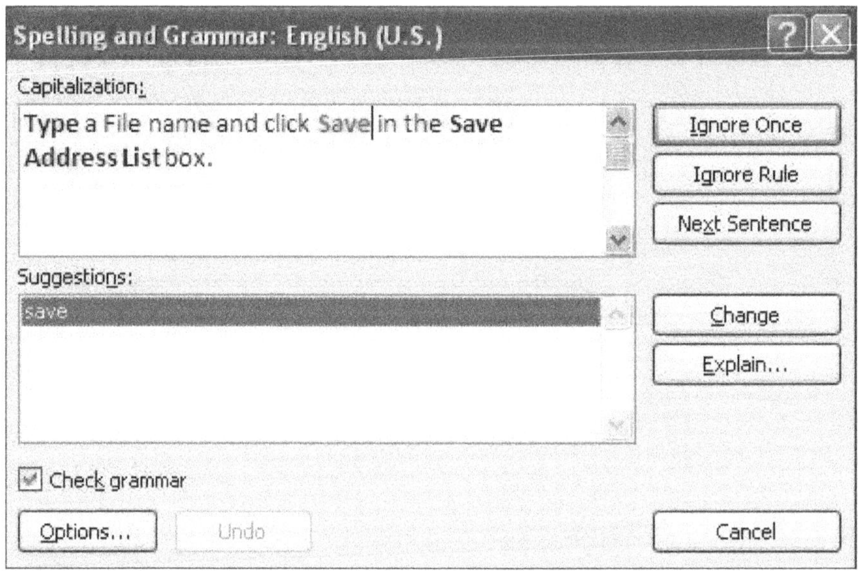

Picture 4.2

3. Click the **Change** button in the **Spelling and Grammar: English (U.S.)** dialog box to replace the correct word with the word in the document.

As the result, the grammatical errors in the document are rectified. The **Spelling and Grammar: English (U.S.)** dialog box contains the following elements:
- **Not in Dictionary:** Refers to the box, which shows the word that was not in the spell checker's dictionary in red.
- **Suggestions:** Refers to the list box that contains all the words that the spell checker has determined and is close to the unknown word. If the word is misspelled, click the suggestion that you want to use as a replacement.
- **Ignore Once:** Refers to the option that allows you to skip the current instance of the word.
- **Ignore All:** Refers to the option that allows you to skip all the instances of the word in the current session.

After clicking the **Change** button in the **Spelling and Grammar: English (U.S.)** dialog box, the Spelling and Grammar feature now search for a new spelling or grammar mistake in the document. Perform the following steps to fix the grammar errors in the document:

1. Click the **Review** tab at the top.

2. Click the **Spelling and Grammar** button in the <u>Proofing</u> group.

The **Spelling and Grammar: English (U.S.)** dialog box appears. If the grammar checker does not find any error, it displays a message box to let you know that the check is complete. Otherwise, it displays the **Spelling and Grammar: English (U.S.)** dialog box. The correct usage of the grammatical mistake in the text is shown in the Suggestions box.

3. Click the correct replacement shown in the **Suggestions** box.

4. Click the **Change** button at the right side.

You can see on your screen that the **Spelling and Grammar: English (U.S.)** dialog box contains the following elements:
- **Grammatical error:** Shows the error in green text. You should check that the name of the box is same as the error category found in the selected text, such as Subject-Verb Agreement.
- **Suggestions:** Allows you to click one of the suggestions that you want to use as a replacement provided by this list box.
- **Ignore Once:** Allows you to skip the current instance of the error.
- **Ignore Rule:** Allows you to skip all instances of the error.
- **Next Sentence:** Allows you to continue the grammar check with the next sentence. This button only indentifies the error and does not fit it.
- **Change:** Allows you to change the erroneous text with the text selected in the Suggestions list.
- **Explain:** Displays a help article that explains the error and offers suggestions to avoid the error.
- **Options:** Displays the Word Option dialog box, which displays the Proofing section.

Selecting a Thesaurus

One of the keys to good writing is using the rich and appropriate vocabulary. If you cannot seem to find the right word, you can use a thesaurus provided in MS Word. Thesaurus is an ultimate tool which provides all the synonyms of a word. Its word choices are fairly limited; however, it provides few quick and handy suggestions. Perform the following steps to use thesaurus in your document:

1. **Select** the word you want to look up for the synonym. In our case, we select the word **difficult**.

2. Click the **Revlew** lab, and click the **Thesaurus** button in the <u>Proofing</u> group, as shown in picture 4.3. It opens the **Research Task** pane.

Alternatively, you can press the Shift+F7 keys. Or else, you can right-click the word and select Synonym and the Thesaurus option. When you click the Thesaurus button, the thesaurus tool appears in the Research pane and looks for the current selected word.

3. Click the **Research Task** pane to look one of the synonyms of word difficult. After looking few words, you can click the Back and Next search buttons in the Research Task pane to navigate your search.

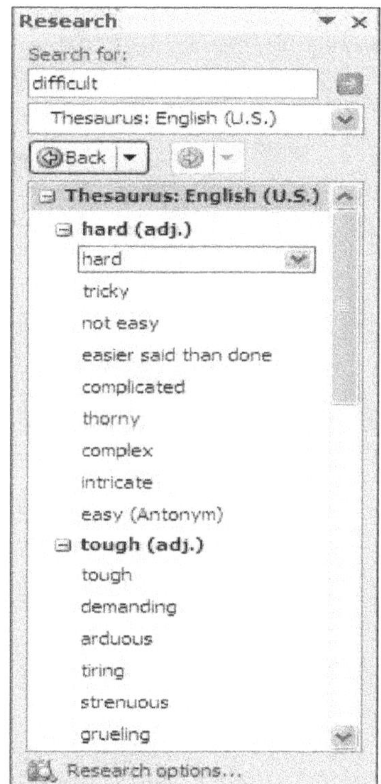

Picture 4.3

4. **Select** a suitable replacement for the word **difficult** and click the dropdown arrow button beside the selected word. In our case, we selected the word **complicated**.

5. Click the **Insert** option from the dropdown list. You can also use the Research pane to look up other information about words. For example, you can use the Research pane to find the types (noun, adjective, and verb) of specified words.

Translating a Document

Many times you must have come across a document or word that was written in a foreign language. However, you may face difficulty in understanding that document or word because neither you are fluent in that foreign language nor you have a personal translator. Microsoft Word 2013 has come up with a solution. It provides the Translation feature with which you can translate words and phrases from one language to another. In addition, you can use this feature to insert translated text in your document. Perform these steps to translate text from one language to another and use it in document:

1. **Select** a word or phrase that you want to translate.

2. Click the **Review** tab, and click the **Translate** button in the <u>Proofing</u> group. It opens the Research pane on the screen.

3. Select a language from the **From** and **To** dropdown lists under the <u>Translation</u> group.

In our case, we select **English** in the **From** dropdown list and **Spanish** in the **To** dropdown list. As the result, the translation appears in the task pane. You may have to scroll down to find the word.

4. **Double-click** a translated word to copy it in your document in the <u>Research</u> pane and select the **Copy** option to copy the word or phrase.

5. **Right-click** the selected word and select the **Paste** option from the shortcut menu to paste it in the file. The translation that you just copied from the Research pane replaces the highlighted word in the document.

If you have an entire document to translate, translating a document word by word at a time is cumbersome. So you can sue the Web-based service to translate an entire document at once. Imagine receiving a 50 page document that needs to be translated. You could be translating the document all week. Follow the given steps to translate an entire document:

1. **Open** the document that you want to translate.

2. Click the **Review** tab, and click the **Research** button in the <u>Proofing</u> group. It opens the Research pane.

3. Click the button under **Translate the whole document** text under <u>Translation</u>.

Your document is sent to a third-party translation service and a translation of the document appears in your Web browser. The main disadvantage to this is that your document is sent across Internet without encryption, which can be a security risk if it contains some sensitive and confidential information.

Lesson 8
Adding Art and Design

MS Word allows you to insert a shape in your document. You can insert ready-made shapes, such as rectangles, circles, arrows, lines, flowcharts symbols and callouts. Perform the following simple steps to insert a shape:

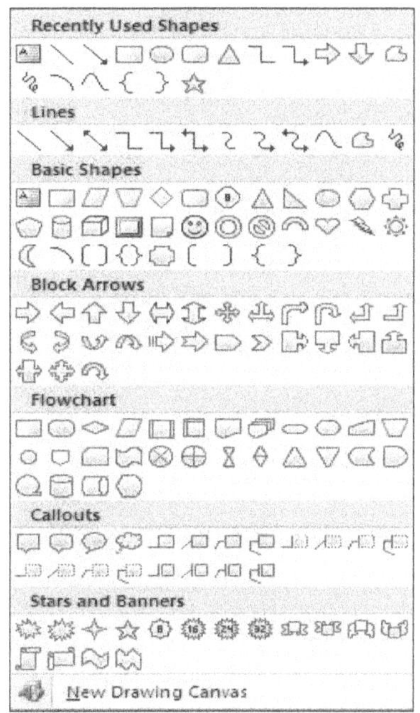

1. **Place** your cursor in the document where you want to insert a shape.

2. Click the **Insert** tab at the top, and click the **Shapes** dropdown button in the <u>Illustrations</u> group in the Ribbon. It opens the Shapes list, as shown in picture 4.4.

3. **Double-click** a shape in the list. As the result, the shape will be inserted in the document.

4. **Select** the inserted shape in your document. Then drag any blue-button handle to enlarge or shorten the shape. You can use the green button to rotate, and yellow button to change the orientation of the shape.

Picture 4.4

When the shape is selected, you will see that **Format** tab at the top is enabled which gives you various options to edit the inserted shape. You can change the style of the shape, fill color, fill outline color, and insert shadow effects and 3D effects in the shape. If you want to delete the inserted shape, you can select the shape and press the Delete key on your keyboard.

Using a Drawing Canvas

When you insert a drawing object in Word, you can place it in a drawing canvas. The drawing canvas helps you arrange a drawing in your document. The drawing canvas provides a frame-like boundary between your drawing and the rest of your document. By default, the drawing canvas has no border or background, but you can apply formatting to the drawing canvas as you would any drawing object. The drawing canvas also helps you keep parts of your drawing together, which is especially helpful if your drawing consists of several shapes. For example, if you want to create a flow chart, you start with a drawing canvas and then add the shapes and lines for your chart. Perform the following steps to place a drawing canvas in your document:

1. Click the **Insert** tab at the top <u>without</u> selecting any inserted shape of your document.

2. Click the **Shapes** dropdown button, and click the **New Drawing Canvas** option at the bottom of the dropdown list. It places the canvas in your document, as shown in picture 4.5.

3. Go to the <u>Insert Shapes</u> group at the top-left corner in the <u>Format</u> tab. Then choose the **Scribble** button in the Insert Shapes group.

4. With the Scribble tool active, **draw** something like the letter **C** in your canvas in the document. It may look like the picture 4.5.

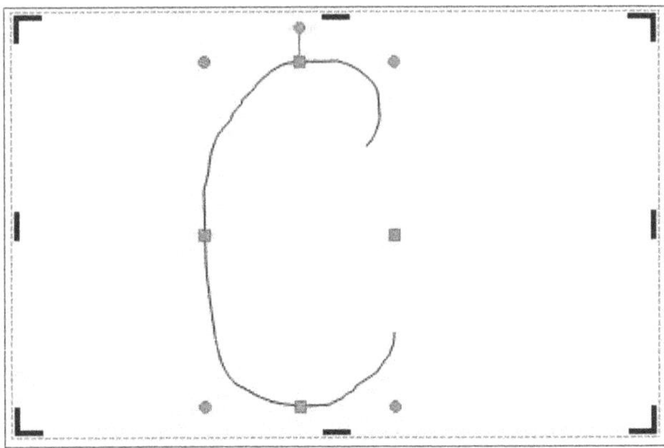

Picture 4.5

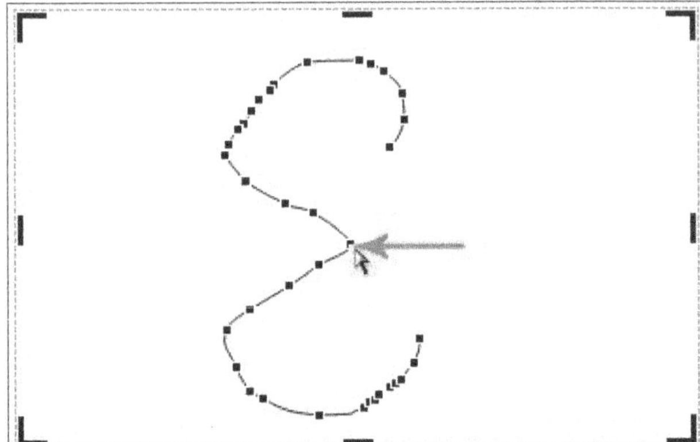

Picture 4.6

5. Click the **Edit Shape** button which is just beside (on the right side) the <u>Insert Shapes</u> group. Then select **Edit Points** from the list it opens.

6. **Drag** any edit point in the canvas to edit the C shape, as shown in picture 4.6. When you are done with the editing, you can click **outside** the canvas. As the result, the edited shape will be inserted in the document.

Inserting a Clip Art

You can insert Clip Arts into your document including drawings, movies, sounds, or stock photography to illustrate a specific concept. Perform the following steps to insert a Clip Art:

1. Click the **Insert** tab at the top, and click **Clip Art** in the Ribbon. It opens the Clip Art pane at the right of the MS Word screen.

2. Click **Organize clips** option at the bottom of the Clip Art pane. It opens the **Favorites – Microsoft Clip Organizer** list box.

3. Go to the **Collection List** which is on the left side in the Microsoft Clip Organizer list box. Then double-click the + sign of **Office Collections** and select **Buildings** option. It opens the Clip Art related to the Buildings option in the list.

4. **Choose** a Clip Art in the list, and **drag and drop** it in your document, as shown in picture 4.7. After the Clip Art is inserted in your document, you can edit it as required.

Picture 4.7

Inserting a Picture

MS Word allows you to insert a picture in your document. Pictures and can be inserted or copied into a document from many different sources, including downloaded from a Web site provider, copied from a Web page, or inserted from a file where you save pictures. You can also change how a picture is positioned with text within a document. Perform the following steps to insert a picture:

1. Click the **Insert** tab at the top, and click **Picture** in the Ribbon. It opens the Insert Picture dialog box on the screen.

2. **Navigate** and **locate** your picture by clicking the option in the Look in section of the Insert Picture dialog box. In our case, we go to **My Documents> My Pictures> Sample Pictures** and select a picture.

3. Click the **Insert** button at the bottom of the dialog box when you have selected a picture. As the result, the picture is inserted in your document where the cursor was placed.

4. Now to position the picture with text in the document, click the **Format** tab at the top when the picture is selected.

5. Click the **Text Wrapping** dropdown button which is in the Arrange group in the Format tab. Then select any option from the dropdown list.

In the Ribbon of the Format tab, there are several options to do various kinds of editing with the picture you have inserted. You can change the brightness, contrast, and style of the picture as you want. If you think this way of inserting a picture is tedious to you, you can directly copy-paste a picture in your Word document. Perform the following steps for this:

1. Go to the **My Documents** folder by clicking the Start button on your desktop.

2. **Select** your picture and press **Ctrl+C** keys to copy.

3. Open your Word document and place the cursor where you want to insert the picture.

4. Press **Ctrl+V** keys to paste the picture in the document.

Using the Draw Text Box

When you insert a picture in the Word document, you may need to write something exactly on the picture you have inserted. For many people, it is a difficult task. In this case, if you know how to draw a text box, you can write your text on the picture easily. Perform the following steps for this:

1. Click the **Insert** tab at the top without selecting the inserted picture of your document.

2. Click the **Shapes** dropdown button, and click the **New Drawing Canvas** option at the bottom of the dropdown list.

3. Go to the Insert Shapes group at the top-left corner in the Format tab. Then click the **Text Box** option which is the very first option in the Insert Shapes group of the Format tab.

4. **Draw** a text box on the picture you have inserted, as shown in picture 4.8.

It is possible that the text box you have drawn is behind the picture, and you are not able to see what you type in the text box. For this, select the picture (not the text box), then right-click on the picture, and then select Send to Back> Send Behind Text. Now you can see what you type in the text box.

5. **Type** a word or sentence in the box. Then you need to click **outside**. In our case, we type Sunrise, as shown in picture 4.8.

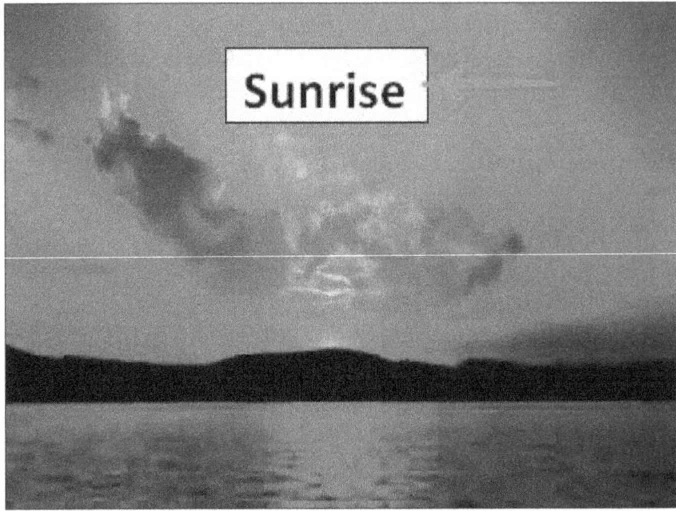

Picture 4.8

Stylize a Picture

MS Word allows you stylize your picture in the document that you have inserted. For example, you can crop, align, rotate, give picture border, and adjust the brightness and contrast of the picture. Perform the following steps to stylize your picture:

1. **Select** the inserted picture in your document.

2. Go to the **Format** tab, and click the **Picture Border** dropdown button in the <u>Picture Styles</u> group.

3. Select the **Weight** option in the dropdown list. Then select the option **6 pt** and click **outside**. You can also crop, align, rotate, and adjust the brightness and contrast of the picture.

Inserting a Picture in a WordArt

I am sure you will like to insert a picture in a WordArt. It gives a magnificent look to the WordArt that you create in the Word document. Perform the following steps for this:

1. **Create** a WordArt and **place** it in the middle of your document.

2. **Select** the WordArt, and click the **Format** tab at the top.

3. Click the **Shape Fill** dropdown button which is just below the Format tab.

4. Select the **Picture** option from the dropdown list. It opens the <u>Select Picture</u> dialog box where you can select your picture to insert in the WordArt.

5. **Navigate** and **select** your picture in the dialog box. Then click the **Insert** button at the bottom of the dialog box. As the result, the face picture is inserted in the WordArt, as shown in picture 4.9.

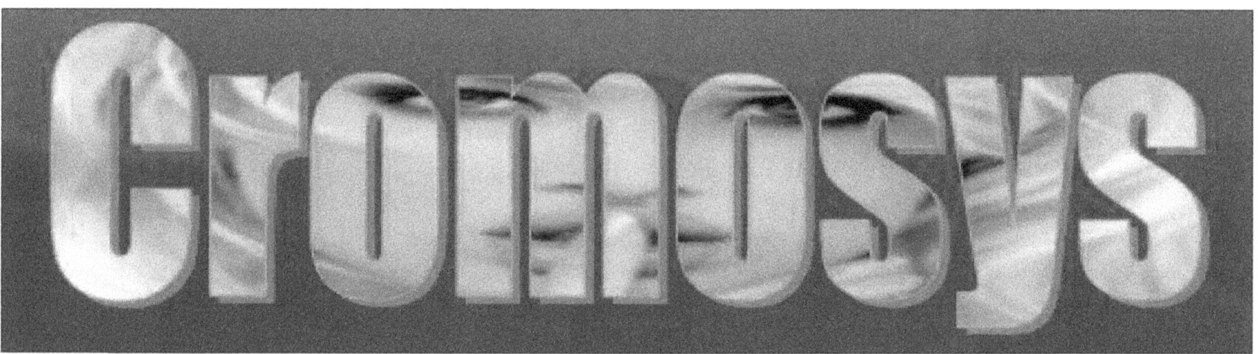

Picture 4.9

Inserting Page Elements

You can insert page number, header, and footer in your Word document. Perform the following simple steps to insert page elements:

1. Click the **Insert** tab at the top of the MS Word window.

2. Click the **Page Number** dropdown button in the Header & Footer group of the Insert tab.

3. Choose the first option: **Top of Page**. Then **select** any option from the list it opens. As the result, it brings the page number on every page of your document.

4. Click the **Footer** dropdown button in the Header & Footer group, and **select** the first option it opens.

5. **Enter** the text that you want to be placed as the footer of your document. Then press **Esc key** on your keyboard.

In this book also, you can see the footer at the end of every page. Similarly, you can also insert the header of your document. To remove the page number, click Remove Page Numbers option under the Page Number dropdown. To remove footer, select Remove Footer option under the Footer dropdown.

Inserting a Chart and SmartArt

Microsoft Word allows you to insert a chart and SmartArt in your document. The chart and SmartArt are very helpful in calculative presentation of your document. Insert a chart to illustrate and compare data. You can use the bar, pie, line, area, and surface chart for this purpose. Perform the following steps to insert a chart:

1. Click the **Insert** tab at the top. It opens the Insert Chart dialog box on your screen.

2. **Choose** any option in the Templates section on the left side of the dialog box.

3. Press the **OK** button at the bottom-right side of the dialog box. It opens the Microsoft Excel program in the half part of your screen.

4. **Enter** the relevant detail in the <u>Excel</u> sheet which is on the right side of your screen. For this, you need to follow the following sub-steps:
   A. First **delete** everything from the column A.
   B. Enter the name of four students in the column A.
   C. **Delete** everything from column B, and **enter** the marks the four students have obtained.
   D. **Delete** everything form column C and D and **close** the Excel page by clicking the X button at the top-right corner of the Excel page.

As the result, the chart is inserted in the MS Word page according to the detail (data) you inserted in the Excel sheet. Let's now insert a SmartArt in a Word document. You can insert a SmartArt graphic to visually communicate information. SmartArt graphics range from graphical lists and process diagrams to more complex graphics, such as Venn diagrams. Perform the following steps to insert a SmartArt:

1. **Open** a new page in MS Word, and click the **Insert** tab at the top.

2. **Select** any art in the **List** section, and click the **OK** button at the bottom.

3. **Enter** the detail in the Smart Art and **change** the color of the SmartArt as per your requirement.

Inserting a Cover

MS Word allows you to insert a fully-formatted cover page for your Word document. You fill in the title, author, date, and other information to complete the cover page. Perform the following steps to insert a cover page:

1. Click the **Insert** tab, and click the **Cover Page** dropdown at the top-left corner.

2. **Select** any cover design from the list it opens. As the result, it inserts the cover for your document.

3. **Edit** the detail in the cover as per your requirement. In case you do not want a cover for your document, you can select **Remove Current Cover Page** option to remove the cover page.

Inserting a Page Break

You can insert a page break anywhere in your document, or you can specify where Microsoft Word positions automatic page breaks. Page break starts the next page at the current location of the cursor blinking in the page. If you insert manual page breaks in documents that are more than several pages in length, you might have to frequently rebreak pages as you edit the document. To avoid the difficulty of manually rebreaking pages, you can set options to control where Word positions automatic page breaks. Perform the following steps to insert a page break:

1. **Type** some text in your Word page.

2. **Place** your cursor at the location where you want to insert page break.

3. Click the **Insert** tab, and click the **Page Break** button. As the result, it breaks the page from where the cursor was placed.

Lesson 9

Creating Form Letters, Email, Messages, and Labels

Form letters, emails, and letters are used to create and send professional documents to multiple clients. Suppose, you work in a publishing house and your job requires you to send business letters to a number of book dealers. However, typing the same letter for different dealers becomes a very tedious job. The solution for this problem lies in a unique and extremely useful feature of Microsoft Word called Mail Merge. When you want to send personalized email to recipients in your address list, you can use mail merge to create the email messages. Each message has the same kind of information, yet the content of each message is unique. Mail Merge helps you in uniquely creating personalized letters for every dealer in your mailing list. You need two documents, such as **Main Document** and **Data Source**, to use Mail Merge. The following points provide brief information about these two documents:

Main Document: Refers to a formatted text file that contains text, such as a business letter you want to send to all book dealers on your mailing list. The Main Document also contains Merge Fields to bring information from your data source at appropriate positions in the document.
Data Source: Contains information, like names, address, and other details of people on your mailing list.

In this chapter, you learn to create a Mail Merge document. You also learn to send a personalized email to multiple clients. Next, you learn to modify records in a Data Source. At the end of the chapter, you learn to create Envelops and Labels. Let's now learn to create a Mail Merge document.

Creating a Mail Merge Document

The process of creating a Mail Merge document starts with deciding the type of main document on which you would work, such as a letter, label, or catalog. Next, you have to collect data for the Data Source. In our case, an invitation letter addressed to all dealers serve as the Main Document. The document or file containing names and addresses of all dealers become the Data Source. In this section, you learn to decide the type of document you are going to create, such as envelop, letter, or label; entering data in a document, creating Data Source and the Main Document, and merging the Main Document with the Data Source. Apart from this, you also learn to print and save the Main Document. Let's go through the procedure to create a Mail Merge project, firstly by deciding the type of document.

Deciding the Type of Document

Suppose you wish to write invitation letters to all your dealers in a given format. The letter should have the various Merge Fields, such as Dealer's First Name, Company Name, Address, City, State, and Reference. The information in these fields varies from dealer to dealer.

Entering Data

Microsoft Words supports many file formats, which can be used as a Data Source for a Mail Merge. Now you learn to insert data in a Mail Merge document performing the following steps:

1. **Open** a new blank page in Microsoft Word.

2. Click the **Mailings** tab at the top. Then click the **Start Mail Merge** button under the Start Mail Merge group.

3. Click the **Step by Step Mail Merge Wizard** option. It opens the Mail Merge Task pane at the right side of the document window. This Task pane has the **Selected document type** category, which lists different types of document.

4. Select the **Letters** radio button in the Mail Merge Task pane. This option enables you to send the invitation letters to all your dealers.

5. Click the **Next: Starting document** link at the bottom of the Task pane. It opens a new Mail Merge Task pane on the screen.

6. Select the **Use the current document** radio button in the Task pane.

7. Click the **Next: Select recipients** option. The Select Recipient option appears on the Mail Merge Task pane.

Now Microsoft Word allows you to set up your letters in three ways. The three options discussed in this section are as follows:
- **Use the current document: Enables you to start from the currently open document and use the Mail Merge to add recipient information.**
- **Start from a template: Enables you to set up your letter by starting a ready-to-use Mail Merge template that can be customized to suit your needs.**
- **Start from existing document: Enables you to start from an existing Mail Merge document and make changes to the contents or recipient. Now, you learn to create the Data Source.**

Creating Data Source

Before you create your Data Source, think about the kinds of information you want to include in your final document. To under the Data Source, first we need to under the data field. The data field is a category of information that corresponds to one column of information in a Data Source. The name of each data field is listed in the first row (header row) of the Data Source. First Name and Last Name are examples of data field names. So this data field in your Data Source corresponds to the Merge Fields. And the Merge field is a placeholder for text or pictures that you insert into your document. Information from a Data Source (such as a name, address, or image) is inserted in each Merge Field. You can format, copy, move, or delete a merge field that you insert into your Mail Merge document. A Data Source must contain all the Merge Fields of the Main Document. However, you must not forget that the format of the invitation letter that forms our Main Document would include the following Merge Fields:

Dealer's First Name Last Name, Company Name, Address, City, State, and Zip code

After inserting the required fields in Data Source, add names and addresses of dealers in it. Data relating to a particular dealer is also known as a record. Perform the following steps on your computer to create Data Source:

1. Open the **Mail Merge** Task pane.

2. Select the **Type a new list** radio button, as shown in picture 5.0. It enables you to create a new list of recipients.

3. Click the **Create** option in the Task pane. The Create option is shown in picture 5.0 with the second arrow.

It opens the <u>New Address List</u> dialog box, in which you can see a number of tabs with their corresponding fields. By default, the cursor appears in the box beside the first field: Title. By the way, the format of the letter (that we have thought) that forms the Main Document does not have any field for Title, so it can be removed.

4. In the <u>New Address List</u> dialog box, click the **Customize Columns** button, as shown in picture 5.1.

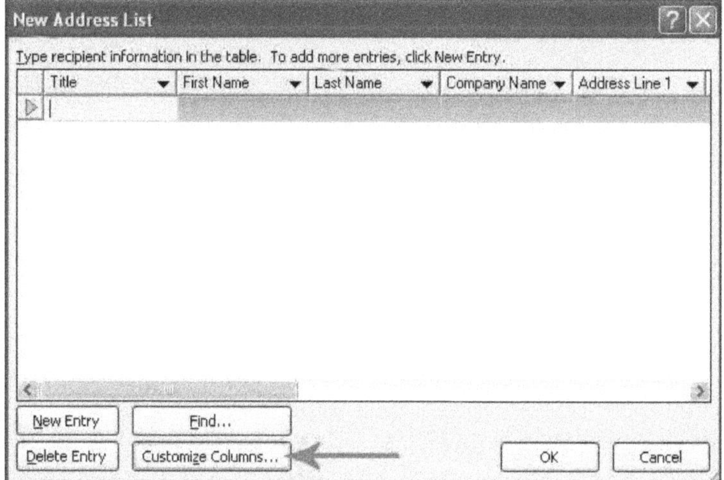

Picture 5.1

When you click the Customize Columns button, it opens the <u>Customize Address List</u> dialog box on the screen, as shown in picture 5.2. This dialog box contains all fields, so that the user could select unwanted fields and remove them. In this dialog box, all the fields are displayed under the Field Name option. By default, the very first field, **Title** appears highlighted. By using the Customize Address List dialog box, you can also remove all those fields which do not serve your purpose. This dialog box allows you to create your own desired field. If required, you can also change the sequential order of fields and rename them.

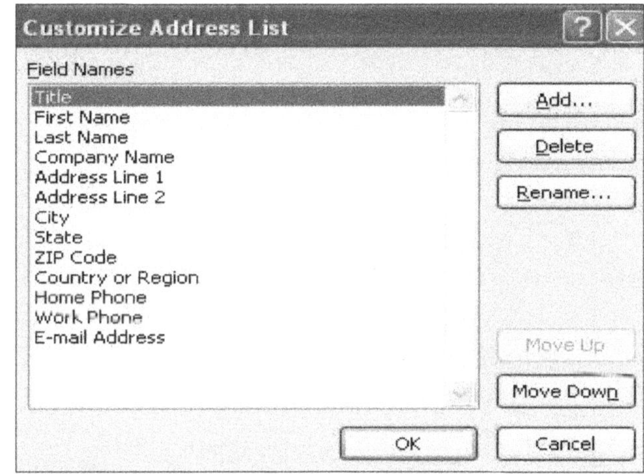

Picture 5.2

5. Click the **Delete** button to remove the <u>Title</u> field from your list. A message box appears on the screen asking whether you want to delete the field. Then click the **Yes** button to delete the Title field. Now the next field: **First Name** gets highlighted in the Customize Address List dialog box.

6. Click the **Address Line 2** field to highlight it. Then click the **Delete** button to delete this filed.

The fields: **City**, **State**, and **Zip Code** are required in the letter whereas the fields: Country, Home Phone, Work Phone, and Email Address can be deleted. So you can remove them in the same manner as explained before. After you delete these extra fields, you are left with the seven fields. However, the Customize Address List dialog box does not have a required field according to the desired letter format and it needs to be created explicitly. The name of such field is Reference. To add an additional field, proceed as follows.

7. Click the **Add** button in the Customize Address List box. It opens the **Add Field** dialog box.

8. Type **Reference** in the box under the Type a name for your field option. Then click the **OK** button in the dialog box. As the result, the Reference field is added to your database and appears in the Customize Address List dialog box in the Field Names option.

9. Click the **OK** button of the Customize Address List dialog box. Now you return to the New Address List dialog box. In this dialog box, you can enter the names and addresses of the dealers to create the required **Data Source** for the **Mail Merge** project.

10. **Click** inside the box under the First Name field. Then type **Mark** as the first name, and press the **Tab** key from the keyboards. The cursor goes inside the box under the Last Name.

11. You need to **type**: Last Name, Company Name, Address Line 1, City, State, Zip Code, and Reference (date) using the tab key.

12. Click the **New Entry** button in the New Address List dialog box. It opens another blank row where you can enter the details of next dealer. Similarly, you can enter information about rest of the dealers in the New Address List dialog box.

13. Click the **OK** button in the New Address List dialog box after adding the details of all the dealers. The Save Address List dialog box appears immediately on the screen.

14. **Type** the name for the address list beside the File name option. In our case, we type **My Books Dealer** as name of the address list.

15. **Click** a location where you want to save the address list in the Navigation Pane. In our case, we click **My Documents** in the Navigation pane.

16. Click the **Save** button of the Save Address List dialog box. The **Mail Merge Recipients** dialog box appears, containing all the information about the dealers in the rows and columns.

17. Click the **OK** button in the Mail Merge Recipients dialog box. It closes the dialog box and displays a blank document on the screen. Let's now learn to create the Main Document.

Creating the Main Document
The Main Document is an invitation that has to be sent to all dealers listed in the mailing list. The mailing list is nothing but a Data Source of different records. Now, you need to type the invitation letter in a blank Word document. While typing the letter, you are required to take care of certain things to convert

the fields selected in the Data Source, into the Merge Fields of the Main Document. When converted into Merge Fields, these fields would automatically replace the individual dealer's address details during the Mail Merge procedure. In other words, Microsoft Word would replace the Merge Fields in the Main Document with the corresponding information from the Data Source. Let's now type the invitation letter performing the following steps:

1. Type **To** from the keyboard inside a blank Word document.

2. Press the **Enter key** twice. Now, let's make First Name a Merge Field.

3. Click the **Mailings** tab at the top, and click the **Insert Merge Field** button in the Write & Insert Fields group.

4. Click the **First Name** field in the dropdown list. The dealer's **First Name** field is inserted as a **Merge Field** in your Main Document. Till now, your Main Document should look like picture 5.3.

To

<<First_Name>>

Picture 5.3

5. Now, we will insert the dealer's **Last Name** as a Merge Field in our Main Document. Press the **Spacebar key** from the keyboard to display the fields: First Name and Last Name together in the invitation letter.

6. Click the **Insert Merge Field** button on the Mailings tab. Then click the **Last Name** field from the dropdown list. When you click, the dealer's Last Name field is also inserted as a Merge Field in our Main Document.

7. Press the **Enter key** once from the keyboard. Then click the **Insert Merge Field** button on the Mailings tab.

8. Click the **Company Name** field. The dealer's Company Name field is inserted as a Merge Field in our Main Document.

9. Press the **Enter key** once from the keyboard. Then click the **Insert Merge Field** button on the Mailings tab.

10. Click the **Address Line 1** field. The dealer's Address Line 1 field is inserted as a Merge Field in our Main Document.

11. Press the **Enter key** once from the keyboard. Then click the **Insert Merge Field** button on the Mailings tab.

12. Click the **City** field. The dealer's City field is inserted as a <u>Merge Field</u> in our Main Document.

13. Press the **Comma** (,) from the keyboard. Then click the **Insert Merge Field** button on the <u>Mailings</u> tab. And then, click the **State** field. The dealer's State field is inserted as a <u>Merge Field</u> in our Main Document.

14. Press the **Enter key** from the keyboard. Then click the **Insert Merge Field** button on the <u>Mailings</u> tab. And then, click the **Zip Code** field. The dealer's State field is inserted as a <u>Merge Field</u> in Main Document.

To,

<<First_Name>><<Last_Name>>

<<Company_Name>>

<<Address_Line_1>>

<<City>><<State>>

<<Zip_Code>>

Sub: With reference to your letter dated <<Reference>>

Dear <<First Name>>

This is to inform you that our company is holding the annual meeting of all the dealers at Hotel Taj Conference Room, Sardar Patel Marg, New Delhi on 5th April 2014. You are requested to attend the meeting at 6 PM sharp. Dinner will be served at 9 PM.

Sincerely,

Ravi Jha

Managing Director

Cromosys Corporation

Picture 5.4

15. Press the **Enter key** twice. Then type **Sub: With reference to your letter dated**. And then, press the **Spacebar key** form the keyboard to give space before the <u>Reference</u> field that we are going to insert.

16. Click the **Insert Merge Field** button on the <u>Mailings</u> tab. Then click the **Reference** field. The Reference field is inserted as a <u>Merge Field</u> in our Main Document.

17. Press the **Enter key** twice, and **type** the salutation text: **Dear**. Then press the **Spacebar key** once from the keyboard to insert a space after the salutation text.

18. Click the **Insert Merge Field** button on the <u>Mailings</u> tab. Then click the **First Name** field. The dealer's First Name field is inserted after the Dear word in our Main Document.

19. Press the **Comma** (,) key once to insert a comma after the <u>First Name</u> field. After that, press the **Enter key**.

20. **Type** the following text of the letter in your document <u>without</u> pressing the Enter key. **This is to inform you that our company is holding the annual meeting of all the dealers at Hotel Taj Conference Room, Sardar Patel Marg, New Delhi on 5th April 2014. You are requested to attend the meeting at 6 PM sharp. Dinner will be served at 9 PM.**

21. Press the **Enter key** four times after typing the text to type the concluding lines of the letter. Then type: **Sincerely** and press the **Comma** (,) key from the keyboard.

22. Press the **Enter key** and type any **name**. Then press the **Enter key** and type the **designation**. And then, press the **Enter key** again and type the **company name**.

Now the letter is completed and already shown in picture 5.4. After this, we need to learn to merge the Main Document with Data Source.

Merging the Main Document with Data Source
After creating the Main Document, you are now ready to combine it with the Data Source to create a personalized letter for each dealer on your mailing list. Perform the following steps to merge the Main Document and Data Source:

1. Click the **Mailings** tab at the top, and click the **Finish & Merge** button in the <u>Finish</u> group.

2. Click the **Edit Individual Document** option from the dropdown list. It opens the <u>Merge to New Document</u> dialog box.

3. Click the **OK** button in the Merge to New Document dialog box. The <u>New Document</u> named **Letter 1** appears on the screen showing all the merged letters. Let's now learn to send the merged document to the printer.

Sending the Merged Document to the Printer
Now you are going to send the merged document to the printer. It means, you can print the letters of all the dealers. Perform the following steps for this:

1. Click the **Mailings** tab at the top, and click the **Finish & Merge** button in the <u>Finish</u> group.

2. Click the **Print Document** option. It opens the <u>Merge to Printer</u> dialog box.

3. Click the **OK** button in the Merge to Printer dialog box. It opens the **Print** dialog box.

There are three options in Print records for different purposes as mentioned here:
- **All: Allows you to print all records in the database.**
- **Current Record: Allows you to print record appearing on the screen.**
- **From: Allows you to print records between a range, such as from record number 2 to 5.**

4. Click the **OK** button to print all the letters. Now we are going to save the document in the next section.

Saving the Main Document

You can save invitation letter or the Main Document for future use. Perform the following steps to save the invitation letter:

1. Click the **Save** button on the Quick Access Toolbar.

2. In the File name option, type: **Invitation Letter**.

3. Click the **Save** button of the Save As dialog box. Let's now learn to send a personalized email message to various persons.

Sending a Personalized Email Message to Multiple Recipients

When you need to send the same information to a large group of people on a list – for example, all your customers, or members of a club or your family – you do not have to print letters and physically mail them. Instead, you can use Mail Merge to create a message that can be sent to a list of email addresses. Perform the following steps on your computer to send an email message to multiple recipients through Mail Merge:

1. **Open** a blank Word document, and click the **Mailings** tab at the top. Then click the **Start Mail Merge** button in the Start Mail Merge group.

2. Click the **Email Message** option from the dropdown list to open the document in the Web Layout view.

3. Click the **Start Mail Merge** button, and click the **Step by Step Mail Merge Wizard** option. It opens the Mail Merge Task pane at the right side of the Word document.

4. Click the **Next: Starting Document** option at the bottom of the Mail Merge Task pane.

5. Click the **Next: Select recipients** option at the bottom of the Mail Merge Task pane.

6. Click the **Select from Outlook Contacts** radio button under Select recipients.

7. Click the **Choose Contacts Folder** option in the Mail Merge Task pane. It opens the Select Contacts dialog box.

8. Click the **OK** button in the Select Contacts dialog box. It opens the **Mail Merge Recipients** dialog box.

9. **Clear** (unselect) the checkbox of those contacts which you do not want to include in the list. Then click the **OK** button in the Mail Merge Recipients dialog box. Now, you return to your document.

10. Click the **Next: Write your email message** option in the Mail Merge Task pane.

11. **Type** your email message (letter) in the Word page. In addition, you need to insert the **Merge Fields** on the appropriate place.

12. Click the **Insert Merge Field** button under Write and Insert Field group on the Mailings tab to insert the Merge Field at the appropriate place on the document. It opens a dropdown list.

13. Click the **first option** in the dropdown list to insert in the document. Similarly, **add** remaining fields in the document.

14. Click the **Next: Preview your document** option in the Mail Merge Task pane.

15. Click the **Next: Complete the merge** option in the Mail Merge Task pane.

16. Click the **Electronic Mail** option in the Mail Merge Task pane. It opens the Merge to Email dialog box.

17. **Write** the subject line in the text box beside the Subject line option, and click the **OK** button.

Now, the email message written in the document has been sent to the respective recipients in the list via email. If you want, you can also view their message in the **Sent Items** of your Microsoft Office Outlook.

Modifying Records in the Data Source

You can add new categories of information to a Data Source — for example, to add Reference number to a client mailing list. You can also delete and rename data fields to match the data they describe. In this section, you learn to add, change, and delete records in a Data Source. Let's now learn to do all these functions one by one.

Adding a New Record

Suppose, a new dealer has recently joined in your business and you want to insert his detail into your Data Source. Perform the following steps to add a new record:

1. Open **Main Document** where you have inserted the Merge Field and created the letter.

2. Click the **Mailings** tab, and click the **Edit Recipient List** button in the Start Mail Merge group. It opens the Mail Merge Recipients dialog box.

3. Click the **My Books Dealer.mbd** option under the Data Source. The Edit button gets highlighted. Then click the **Edit** button at the bottom-left corner.

4. Click the **New Entry** button to add details of a new dealer. An empty row for the new record gets inserted in the Edit Data Source dialog box.

5. **Type** the relevant information under each column heading in the Edit Data Source dialog box. Then click the **OK** button after filling up all the details. A message box appears to confirm the modification in the existing list.

6. Click the **Yes** button in the message box. Then click the **OK** button in the <u>Mail Merge Recipients</u> dialog box after confirming the insertion of new entry. As the result, the Data Source is updated in the Main Document.

7. Click the **Mailings** tab to view the invitation letter of the new record. Then click the **Preview Results** button in the <u>Preview Results</u> group.

8. Click the **Last Record** button in the <u>Preview Results</u> group to view the last record. Let's now change an existing record.

Changing an Existing Record

If the address of a particular dealer changes, you also need to make corresponding changes in that dealer's record in your Data Source. Perform the following steps for this:

1. Open the **Main Document** in which letter has been written and **Merge Fields** are inserted.

2. Click the **Mailings** tab, and click the **Edit Recipient List** button in the Start Mail Merge group.

3. Click the **My Books Dealer.mbd** option under the <u>Data Source</u> in the Mail Merge Recipients dialog box. The Edit button gets highlighted. Then click the **Edit** button at the bottom-left corner.

4. Click the box under the **Address Line 1** column to change the Address Line 1 of the dealer. Then press the **Delete key** to delete the text in the Address Line 1 field.

5. **Enter** the new address of the dealer. Then click the **OK** button in the <u>Edit Data Source</u> dialog box. A message box appears to confirm the modification of the new entry.

6. Click the **Yes** button in the message box. Now you can see the modified entry in the Mail Merge Recipients dialog box.

7. Click the **OK** button in the Mail Merge Recipients dialog box. As the result, the <u>Data Source </u>is updated in the Main Document. Let's now learn to delete an existing record in the next section.

Deleting an Existing Record

You have ended your business relationship with a particular dealer and you want to delete his record from your Data Source. Suppose you want to delete the last record in the dealer's document. Perform the following steps to do so:

1. Open the **Main Document** in which letter has been written and **Merge Fields** are inserted.

2. Click the **Mailings** tab, and click the **Edit Recipient List** button in the Start Mail Merge group.

3. Click the **My Books Dealer.mbd** option under the <u>Data Source</u> in the Mail Merge Recipients dialog box. The Edit button gets highlighted. Then click the **Edit** button at the bottom-left corner.

4. **Select** the record that you want to delete. Then click the **Delete Entry** button in the <u>Edit Data Source</u> dialog box. A message box appears asking for confirmation.

5. Click the **Yes** button in the message box. Then click the **OK** button in the Edit Data Source dialog box to save the changes. Again the message box appears asking you whether you want to update the **Data Source** or not.

6. Click the **Yes** button in the message box. Then click the **OK** button in the <u>Mail Merge Recipients</u> dialog box. Let's now learn to create envelops and labels.

Envelopes and Labels

We live in email world nowadays, which means that most of our written communication is delivered electronically. However, this does not indicate that hard copy messages are obsolete. Many of us still rely on post office for the delivery of bills, bill payments, statements, resumes, letters, and many other forms of correspondence. When you need your letters via snail mail method, you need to take care that the language of the letters is accurate and easy to understand. Simply writing a name and address on the front of an envelop might be quick, but it is not a good idea for two reasons:

- The post office or the recipient might misread the address and deliver the envelope to the wrong person or location.
- The handwritten address does not create your good impression on the recipient, as it looks unprofessional.

However, you can avoid these problems by creating envelopes and labels in MS Word. This ensures a neat and accurate address on the front of the envelope. In addition, it is easier to add return address and graphics on letters in MS word. Let's begin this section by learning the process of creating an envelope.

Creating an Envelope

When you have taken the time and trouble to create a professional letter or other document for mailing, you do not have to spoil the good impression with a hand written envelope. Microsoft Word makes it easy for you to create a professional envelope. Perform the following steps to create an envelope:

1. **Open** a blank document, and click the **Mailings** tab at the top.

2. Click the **Envelopes** button in the <u>Create</u> group. It opens the **Envelopes and Labels** dialog box.

3. **Type** the address in the <u>Delivery address</u> box. Then, you can **type** the return address in the **Return address** box (if needed).

4. Click the **Print** button to print the envelope.

If you want to print the envelope along with the document later on, you can insert the envelope into the document by clicking the Add to Document button.

MS Word adds a new page to the top of the document (by inserting a page break) and displays the return and mailing addresses. Later on, you can print the envelope and document by clicking the Print option I the Office Button dropdown list.

If this is the first time you have specified a return address, MS Word displays a message box asking whether you want to save it as the default return address or not.

Envelopes come in different sizes, from the default "size 10" envelope (4 1/8 inches x 9 1/2 inches) to letter (8 ½ by 11) to legal (8 ½ by 14). The size of the envelope determines where MS Word prints the addresses, so if you using anything other than the default size envelope, you need to specify which size you are using. Perform the following steps to change the size of the envelope:

1. Click the **Mailings** tab, and click the **Envelopes** button in the <u>Create</u> group. It opens the **Envelopes and Labels** dialog box.

2. Click the **Options** button in the Envelopes and Labels dialog box. Then click the **Envelope size** list down arrow button.

3. **Click** the appropriate envelope type from the dropdown. Then click the **OK** button in the <u>Envelope Options</u> dialog box.

4. Click the **Print** or **Change Document** button in the <u>Envelopes and Labels</u> dialog box. In our case, we have clicked the **Change Document** button.

In case, you try to edit Envelope in the Document, the Change Document button appears in the Envelope and Labels dialog box. If you are working with a document that already contains the envelope, click on the Change Document button, instead. The Envelope appears in the document with the size you have chosen in the Envelope Options dialog box.

Creating Labels

Instead of printing and address directly on an envelope, you can place the address on a label and then stick the label on the envelope. This process is useful if you are using large sized envelopes or if you are using padded envelopes that could jam the printer. In addition, labels can be used as name tags on disks and file folders. Perform the following steps to create labels:

1. Click the **Mailings** tab, and click the **Labels** button in the <u>Create</u> group. It opens the **Envelopes and Labels** dialog box.

2. **Type** the address in the <u>Address</u> box. The <u>Label</u> group shows the currently selected label.

3. Click the **Options** button in the Envelopes and Labels dialog box to change the label. It opens the **Label Option** dialog box.

The print group gives you the following options:
- **Full page of the same label: Allows you to fill the page with multiple labels.**
- **Single label: Allows you to print only one label. Use the Row and Column spin boxes to specify where you want the label printed.**

4. **Scroll** through the Product number list to select the appropriate label type. Every label type has a different height, width, and page size. You can resize the label as per your requirement.

5. Click the **OK** button in the Label Options dialog box. The Envelops and Labels dialog box reappears.

6. Click the **Print** button in the dialog box to print the label. With this, we come to the end of this chapter.

Lesson 10
Using AutoCorrect

You may have seen several times that MS Word automatically corrects some words in the document as you type. It happens because of AutoCorrect settings in MS Word. AutoCorrect formats the word as you type. For words or symbols, you can set the combination keys in AutoCorrect, which in result will type the entire word or symbol as you press the combination keys on your keyboard. Perform the following steps to set the AutoCorrect combination keys:

1. **Open** a blank document, and click the **Office Button** at the top-left corner.

2. Click the **Word Options** button in the list of Office Buttons.

3. Click the **Proofing** button at the left in the Word Options dialog box. Then click the **AutoCorrect Options** link button in the middle. It opens the **AutoCorrect: English (U. S.)** dialog box.

4. In Replace text box, type: **c?.**

5. In With text box, type: **company**. Then click the **OK** button at the bottom.

6. In your MS Word document, now type: **c?**, and press the **Spacebar key**. As the result, it will automatically replace the c? with **company**.

This kind of tags is set in AutoCorrect for typing convenience, but setting too many unnecessary tags may create problems in typing.

Using Page Color

If required, you can set the page color of your Word document. It means, you can fill color in the background of the page. This option also allows you to insert gradient, texture, pattern, and picture in the background. Perform the following steps for this:

1. Click the **Page Layout** tab at the top, and click the **Page Color** dropdown button.

2. **Select** a color from the list of colors, and click the **OK** button. As the result, the selected color is set as the page color.

You can also insert a picture instead of color in the page background. For that, you need to click the Fill Effects button in the Page Color dropdown. Then click the Picture tab, and select a picture.

Setting Page Border

MS Word also allows you to set page border for your document. it will insert the border in the page you are working on. Here are the steps to perform:

1. Click the **Page Layout** tab, and click the **Page Border** button.

2. Click the **Page Borders** tab at the top, and **choose** a border in the <u>Style</u> section.

3. Click the **OK** button at the bottom. It will show the border in the page you are working on.

Using Water Mark

Using this option, you can put a small part of your text in gray color which prevents the confidential document from being copied (Xerox) after printing. Here are the steps to perform:

1. Click the **Watermark** dropdown button under the <u>Page Layout</u> tab.

2. **Select** the first option in the list. If you want to change the text of the watermark, you need to select the <u>Custom Watermark</u> option.

Direct Cut and Paste Command

Windows operating system allows you to direct copy-and-paste your file from one folder to another. It saves your time of opening the file and saving it again using the Save As option. Perform the following steps to under it practically:

1. **Create** two folders in your <u>My Documents</u> folders.

2. **Name** these two folders: **Folder One**, and **Folder Two**. You can do this by right-clicking on the folder and selecting Rename option.

3. **Create** a document in MS Word, and **save** it in <u>Folder One</u> with the name **My File**.

4. **Close** MS Word, and **open** My Documents folder by clicking the <u>Start</u> button on your desktop.

5. **Open** Folder One, **select** My File document, and press **Ctrl+X** to cut the document. Then **close** the <u>Folder One</u> folder.

6. **Open** Folder Two, and press **Ctrl+V** to paste the document you had cut. It removes the My File document from Folder One and pastes in Folder Two. To be sure of what it has done, you can open both of the folders and see the location of the document.

If you want to make a copy of My File document and do not want to remove it from Folder One, you need to press Ctrl+C keys instead of Ctrl+X. In case you want to rename your document (file) without deleting it, then right-click on the file-icon in Folder One, and select Rename. After that, enter a new name of the file and click outside. It automatically saves your file with the new name.

Publishing to PDF

PDF is a fixed-layout electronic file format that preserves document formatting and enables file sharing. The PDF format ensures that when the file is viewed online or printed, it retains exactly the format that you intended, and that data in the file cannot easily be changed. This process also bitmaps the text that can not be embedded. To view a PDF file, you must have a PDF reader named **Adobe Acrobat Reader** installed in your computer. Perform the following steps to publish a Word document to PDF format:

1. **Create** a file in MS Word application.

2. Click the **Office Button**, go to **Save As**, and select **PDF or XPS** option.

3. **Enter** the file name, and click the **Publish** button at the bottom. It saves the file in PDF format at the location you have selected.

After the file is saved, it automatically opens the file in Adobe Acrobat Reader. In case it does not open the file, you can double-click the PDF file icon. As said earlier, to read this file in PDF format, you should have **Adobe Acrobat Reader** installed in your computer.

Lesson 11
Protecting Your Document

Microsoft Word 2013 allows you to protect your document with password, so that no one can change the content of your document. Perform the following steps for this:

1. **Create** a document in MS Word, and click the **Review** tab at the top.

2. Click the **Protect Document** dropdown button at the top-right side in the Ribbon.

3. In the dropdown list, select the first option: **Restrict Formatting and Editing**.

4. Select the second option: **Allow only this type of editing** with <u>No changes (Read only)</u> option selected.

5. Click the button: **Yes, Start Enforcing Protection** at the bottom.

6. Type your **password** in both of the password boxes. Make sure you type the same password in both of the boxes. And, do not forget your password; otherwise your file will be lost forever.

7. Click the **OK** button, and **save** this file. Now, if you try to edit this file by typing something else in it, MS Word will not allow you to do that.

Unprotect Your Document

You can unprotect the protected document and start editing the content of it. Perform the following steps for this:

1. In the same <u>Restrict Editing and Formatting</u> panel, click **Stop Protection** button at the bottom.

2. Type your **password** and click the **OK** button. Now, it will allow you to edit your document.

Locking Your Document

You can lock your Word file completely so that no one can even open it. But before you move ahead with this command, do not forget the password you enter, and do not misuse this command to damage the documents of other people. Here are the steps to perform:

1. **Create** and **Save** your Word document.

2. Click the **Office Button**, choose **Prepare**, and select **Encrypt Document**.

3. **Type** your password, and click the **OK** button. **Re-enter** your password, and click the **OK** button.

4. **Save** this document again, and **close** MS Word application. Now double-click on this file's icon to open it in MS Word. It will ask the password to open. To proceed further, you can **enter** your password and click the **OK** button.

Unlocking Your Document

You can unlock the same document that you have encrypted with password. If you want to remove the password of the document you have locked, you can perform the following steps carefully:

1. **Open** the same (locked) document entering the correct password.

2. Click the **Office Button**, choose **Prepare**, and select **Encrypt Document**.

3. **Delete** the password from the password box, and click the **OK** button.

4. **Save** the document (must), and **close** Word program. Now you can open this file without entering the password.

Locking Your Entire Folder Permanently

You can lock your entire folder in Windows so that no one can see what the folder contains. When you lock your folder, it is compressed, and it will not even give the thumbnail preview of the files it contains. Do not forget your password, and do not misuse this command. Keep in mind that you cannot reverse back this command after it is executed. It is advisable that you should try this command only on the folder that you want to be locked (compressed) permanently. This process deletes your original folder and replaces it with the compressed (exact copy) folder. If you want, you can keep a copy of your original folder at some other location or in other computer. Perform the following steps to lock your entire folder permanently:

1. **Create** a folder on your desktop, and **put** some Word files and picture files (JPEG pictures) in it.

2. **Right-click** the folder, choose **Properties**, and click the **Advanced** button under <u>General</u> tab.

3. Select the option: **Encrypt Contents to data source**, and click the **OK** button.

4. Click **Apply** and click the **OK** button again. It will take sometime to process encryption.

5. **Right-click** the folder, choose **Send To**, and select **Compressed (Zipped) folder**. It creates a duplicate compressed (copy) of the folder.

6. **Double-click** the compressed (copy) folder to open. It opens the folder in a new window.

7. In the new window, click the **File** tab at the top in the Menu bar, and select **Add a Password** option.

8. **Type** your password (same) two times, and click the **OK** button.

9. **Delete** the original (un-compressed) folder from your desktop. It you want, you can copy this folder to other location before you delete it.

After you delete the original folder, you see only the compressed folder on your desktop. Now, when you try to open the Word files and JPEG pictures of this folder, it will ask the password for each file. The more interesting thing is that this folder will not even show the thumbnail preview of the contents.

Saving Document as Web Page

You can save your Word document as a Web Page. Once you save it as a Web page, you can upload this page on your website using the website building software, such as Adobe Dreamweaver. After this page is uploaded on your website, you can open this file in Internet Explorer. Perform the following steps to save the Word document as a Web page:

1. **Create** a Word file, and click the **Save As** button under Office Button.

2. Select **Other Formats** option in Save As list.

3. **Enter** the file name, and select **Web Page** under Save as type dropdown list.

4. Click the **Save** at the bottom. It saves your document in HTML code which can be viewed on Internet browser.

Now, if you double-click your file which is saved in Web Page format, it will open the file in Internet Explorer on your computer even if you do not have Internet connection. In this process, MS Word also creates some other code files which are used at the time of uploading the document on a website.

Saving Document as Plain Text

Sometimes, when you open a Word file, you see the text formatted in different styles which distract you from reading the file. In this case, you can save this file as a plain text to read. Perform the following steps for this:

1. **Open** a Word file which has the text in different styles.

2. Select **Save As** under Office Button, and click **Other Formats**.

3. **Enter** the file name, and select **Plain Text** under Save as type dropdown list.

4. Click the **Save** button at the bottom. As the result, it saves the document as a plain Notepad file removing all the format-styles and pictures. You can open this file in Notepad to read.

Doing Print Screen

Windows operating system allows you to take a snapshot of what is open on your monitor screen. You can take a snapshot of text file, picture, or website and save it in Microsoft Paint program. Perform the following steps for this:

1. **Open** a picture (or text) on your monitor screen.

2. Press the **Print Screen** key on your keyboard which is beside the F12 key on your keyboard. The Print Screen key captures the screenshot.

3. **Open** the Microsoft Paint program. Then press **Ctrl+V** to paste the screenshot in the Paint program.

4. Select **Save As** in the File tab in Microsoft Paint.

5. **Enter** the name of this file (picture), and select **JPEG** in the Save as type dropdown list. It saves the screenshot as a picture file in your computer.

Niranjan Jha Showman
Trainer, Author, Physician, Entrepreneur, Filmmaker, Activist
Cromosys Corporation
Education and Technology Research Center
www.facebook.com/cromosys
+91-9561450045
Nallasopara (W), Mumbai, India

NIRANJAN JHA SHOWMAN

Founder - Niranjan Jha Showman

Corporation

Education and Technology Research Center

Patankar Park, Nallasopara (W), Mumbai. +91-9561450045

Education, Technology, Publication, Healthcare, Newsmedia, Realtor, Filmmaking

www.facebook.com/cromosys

Cromosys Publication
Teach
Yourself
German
NIRANJAN JHA SHOWMAN

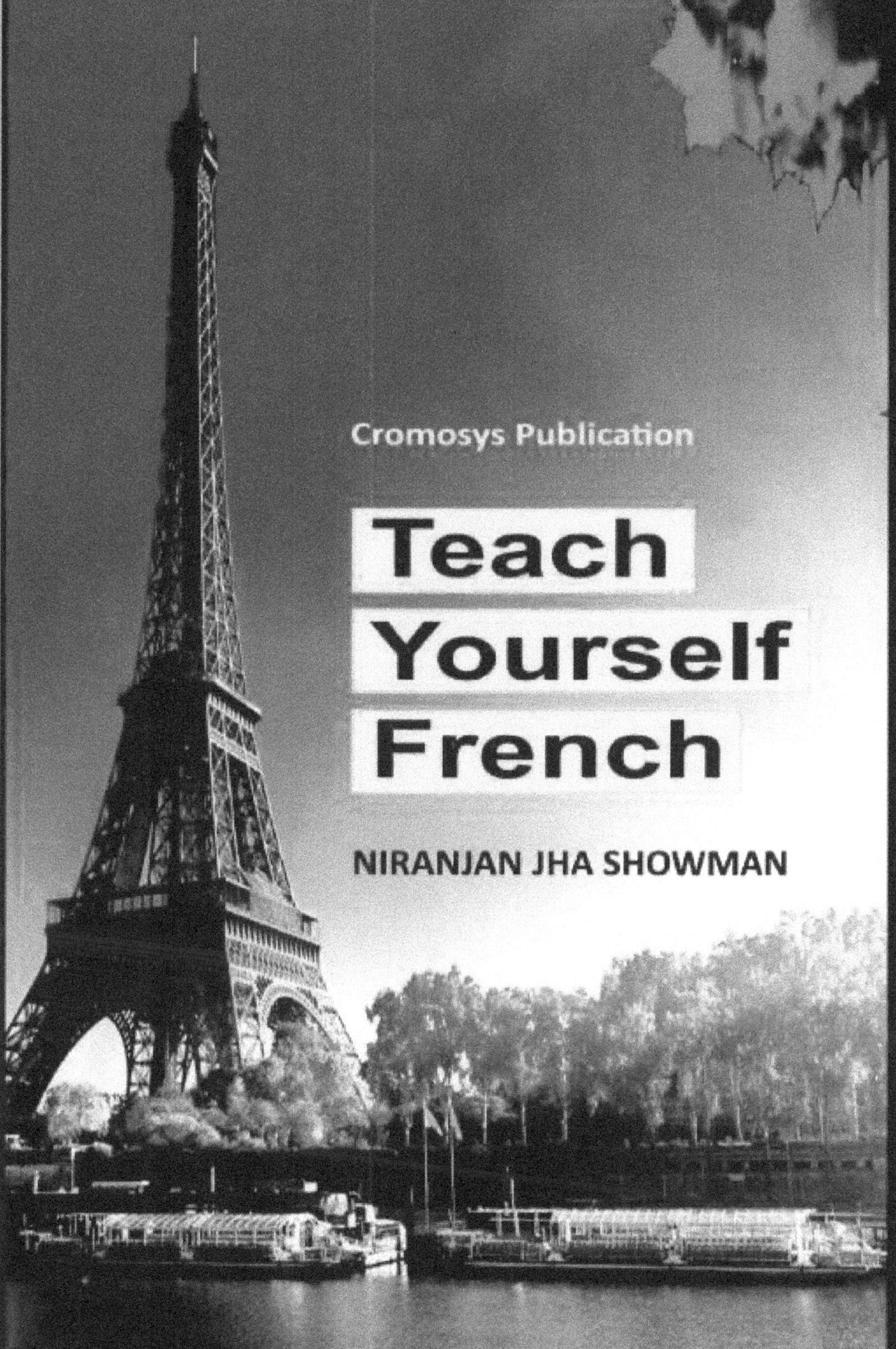

Cromosys Publication

Teach
Yourself
French

NIRANJAN JHA SHOWMAN

Cromosys Publication

Teach
Yourself
Spanish

NIRANJAN JHA SHOWMAN

Cromosys Publication

English
Voice
Accent and
Pronunciation

NIRANJAN JHA SHOWMAN

Teach
Yourself
Autodesk
MAYA
Cromosys Publication
NIRANJAN JHA SHOWMAN

Cromosys Publication

Teach
Yourself
Autodesk
3ds Max

NIRANJAN JHA SHOWMAN

Cromosys Publication
CRIMINAL FACTORY
NIRANJAN JHA SHOWMAN

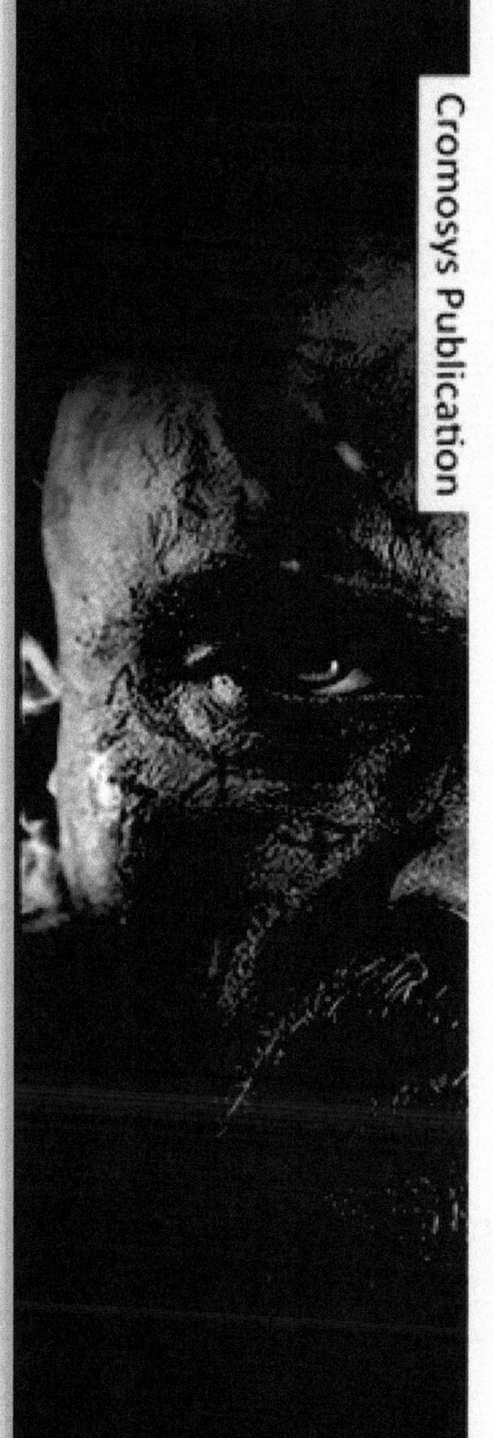

Cromosys Publication
FOCAL DISASTER
NIRANJAN JHA SHOWMAN

Cromosys Publication
Your talents will not help you succeed without your skill of using them.
NIRANJAN JHA SHOWMAN
BE
MILLIONAIRE
LIKE
ME

Copyright Office
Government of India

सत्यमेव जयते

Extracts
from the Register
of Copyrights

Dated : 16/08/2022

1.	Registration Number	:	**T-85782-2022**
2.	Name, address and nationality of the applicant	:	NIRANJAN JHA SHOWMAN, CROMOSYS PUBLICATION, 001, JAYSATYAM, PATANKAR ROAD, NALLASOPARA (W), MUMBAI, MAHARASHTRA - 401203. INDIAN
3.	Nature of the applicant's interest in the copyright of the work	:	AUTHOR
4.	Class and description of the work	:	LITERARY / BOOK
5.	Title of the work	:	**Teach Yourself Word**
6.	Language of the work	:	ENGLISH
7.	Name, address and nationality of the author and if the author is deceased, date of his decease	:	NIRANJAN JHA SHOWMAN, CROMOSYS PUBLICATION, 001, JAYSATYAM, PATANKAR ROAD, NALLASOPARA (W), MUMBAI, MAHARASHTRA - 401203. INDIAN
8.	Whether the work is published or unpublished	:	UNPUBLISHED
9.	Year and country of first publication and name, address and nationality of the publisher	:	N.A.
10.	Years and countries of subsequent publications, if any, and names, addresses and nationalities of the publishers	:	N.A. SAME AS ABOVE
11.	Names, addresses and nationalities of the owners of various rights comprising the copyright in the work and the extent of rights held by each, together with particulars of assignments and licences, if any	:	
12.	Names, addresses and nationalities of other persons, if any, authorised to assign or licence of rights comprising the copyright	:	N.A.
13.	If the work is an 'Artistic work', the location of the original work, including name, address and nationality of the person in possession of the work. (In the case of an architectural work, the year of completion of the work should also be shown).	:	N.A.
14.	If the work is an 'Artistic work', whether it is registered under the Designs Act 2000 if yes give details.	:	N.A.
15.	If the work is an 'Artistic work', capable of being registered as a design under the Designs Act 2000,whether it has been applied to an article though an industrial process and ,if yes ,the number of times it is reproduced.	:	N.A.
16.	Remarks, if any	:	

Diary Number :   8323/2020-DF/T
Date of Application :   25/07/2020
Date of Receipt :   25/07/2020

DEPUTY REGISTRAR OF COPYRIGHTS

Cromosys Publication

Teach Yourself Microsoft WORD

NIRANJAN JHA SHOWMAN